Educating for Redemptive Community

Educating for Redemptive Community

Essays in Honor of Jack Seymour and Margaret Ann Crain

Denise Janssen, editor

Foreword by
Mary Elizabeth Moore

WIPF & STOCK · Eugene, Oregon

EDUCATING FOR REDEMPTIVE COMMUNITY

Wipf & Stock
An Imprint of Wipf and Stock Publishers
199 W. 8th Ave., Suite 3
Eugene, OR 97401

www.wipfandstock.com

ISBN 13: 978-1-4982-0816-1

Manufactured in the U.S.A.   09/30/2015

The authors and editor have made every effort to trace the ownership of all quotes. In the event of a question arising from the use of a quote, we regret any error made and will be pleased to make the necessary correction in future printings and editions of this book.

Unless otherwise noted, all scripture quotations are from the New Revised Standard Version of the Bible, © 1989, Division of Christian Education of the National Council of Churches of Christ in the United States of America, and are used by permission.

To Margaret Ann and Jack, with gratitude.

Your gracious teaching, your prophetic scholarship, your whole lives embody redemptive love and point the way to redemptive community.

YOU are gifts of grace!

Table of Contents

Contributors

Dori Grinenko Baker, Theologian-in-Residence, Forum for Theological Exploration, Atlanta, Georgia

Reginald Blount, Assistant Professor of Formation, Youth, and Culture, Garrett-Evangelical Theological Seminary, Evanston, Illinois

Margaret Ann Crain, Professor Emerita of Christian Education, Garrett-Evangelical Theological Seminary, Evanston, Illinois

Carmichael Crutchfield, Assistant Professor of Christian Education and Youth Ministry, Memphis Theological Seminary, Memphis, Tennessee

Leah Gunning Francis, Assistant Professor of Christian Education, Associate Dean of Contextual Education, Eden Theological Seminary, St. Louis, Missouri

Denise Janssen, Assistant Professor of Christian Education, Samuel De-Witt Proctor School of Theology, Virginia Union University, Richmond, Virginia

Débora B.A. Junker, Assistant Dean of Student Life, Director of the Office of International Students, and Director of the Hispanic Center, Garrett-Evangelical Theological Seminary, Evanston, Illinois

Mary Elizabeth Moore, Dean and Professor of Theology and Education, Boston University School of Theology, Boston, Massachusetts

CONTRIBUTORS

Evelyn L. Parker, Professor of Practical Theology, Associate Dean for Academic Affairs, Perkins School of Theology, Southern Methodist University, Dallas, Texas

Jack L. Seymour, Professor Emeritus of Religious Education, Garrett-Evangelical Theological Seminary, Evanston, Illinois

Mai-Anh Le Tran, Associate Professor of Christian Education, Eden Theological Seminary, St. Louis, Missouri

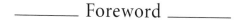

Foreword

A Gift of Redemptive Love

Mary Elizabeth Moore

Why do former students, who are also colleagues and friends, write a book to honor their teachers? This is an act of grateful love—an act that testifies to the bounteous gifts of their teachers, who have touched and transformed their lives and walked with them into new paths of scholarship and leadership. Gratitude is a holy practice that reveals the hearts of the ones who are grateful and the hearts of those for whom the gratitude is intended. The spirit of grateful love lies at the heart of this book, and it flows from every page. Jack Seymour and Margaret Ann Crain quote their colleagues and former students, and they quote one another. All of the authors point to a love, imbued with appreciation and aimed toward redemption. This love is a gift from God; it is a response to God's initiating love and to God's call to redemptive living. It is a testimony to the power of redemption and to the real possibility of education for redemptive community. What a hopeful, yet daunting, claim!

The authors of this book have completed their chapters during a year of horrific violence in the United States and in the world. It is year when Korea continues to be divided into two countries in spite of valiant efforts to build human and political relationships; it is a year when Israelis and Palestinians still search for just peace. It is a year when climate change has escalated and the destruction of the earth's resources and atmosphere has reached very close to the point of irreversibly destroying our entire planet. The violence of oppression and attacks on human persons are raging on every continent; many black lives have been stolen in acts of violence in the U.S.; racial prejudices and injustices appear in horrific acts of murder, including the killing of nine people in the Emanuel African Methodist Episcopal Church in Charleston, South Carolina. Every morning's news brings a new cause for alarm, and the bad news generates diverse responses, some of which produce more bad news. In this one year, we have witnessed responses of rage, nonviolent protest on the streets of Ferguson and Baltimore, violent responses in streets across the U.S., peace talks and trade talks, ecological marches, and undeserved offers of forgiveness and prayer from family members and congregants toward the man accused of slaying their loved ones in the weekly Bible study at Mother Emanuel Church. This is the world to which this book is written. It is a world that longs for redemption.

But what is the redemption that the authors seek? Traditionally, redemption has been understood as a process of buying back, recovering, reclaiming, retrieving, or returning. It is a process of clearing a debt, atoning for sin, honoring a promise, or fulfilling an obligation. In all of these classic definitions, it has to do with something that was lost or gone awry being recovered or set straight. In the Christian tradition, it usually refers to salvation from sin and evil and/or salvation to a better, more faithful and whole, way of life, whether for individuals or for whole communities. The authors of this book identify redemption in more than one way, but they recognize that much has been lost or has gone terribly awry in this world and that the world is in need of redemption—redemption *from* the horrors of injustice and violence, and redemption *to* righteousness, justice, and peace. Further, they are convinced that education can be a pathway of redemption; it can transform human lives, indeed all of God's creation, from destruction and death into life. It can be a pathway for honoring the dignity of every being in God's cosmos and cultivating the goodness and beauty in every living soul and in the whole of God's creation. Education is thus a means of grace.

This book is born in redemptive love, as embodied in the authors who all know and value Jack Seymour and Margaret Ann Crain. They are themselves motivated by love, but they also point to redemptive love as a real possibility that can be nurtured and shaped through education. The authors point vividly to the brokenness of God's creation, and simultaneously to the potential of redemptive love to heal and repair—to lean toward the vision sowed by God of a New Creation in the making. This potential is fed by four currents or recurring themes to which I now turn.

Centering on Bold Visions—The Promise of Paying Attention

The book opens with the bold claim of Margaret Ann Crain, one of the honorees: "I have tried to empower clergy and laity to be co-creators with God in the redemption of creation." However, Margaret Ann quickly adds the sober recognition that the world is still "torn apart by injustice, oppression, and violence." Her awareness of the devastations that live on in the world is testimony to the boldness of her efforts to empower people in the work of co-creating and redeeming. To empower people for redemptive work when one expects good results is a high calling and holy response, but to empower people for redemptive work when the results are not guaranteed is courageous and bold. For Margaret Ann Crain, this pathway is marked by trusting in God's promises and following God's call, even when the rewards are uncertain and the positive outcomes seem meager at best. For Margaret Ann Crain, redemption is *in the process*; it is not an outcome, but is a *walk with God in community with others*. Such a walk requires deep listening and astute observation; thus, Crain conducts her naturalistic ethnography research with the very practices of listening and observing that befit her goals of revealing God and God's hopes for the world. Both the processes and goals of research are redemptive, and both are critical to her faith journey and to that of the Christian community.

Building on the theme of listening and seeing, Jack Seymour invites people to "pay attention." Indeed, educating for redemptive community is a process of learning to pay attention, which includes "praying for relief, challenging principalities and powers, and working for community." It also includes "looking for and following the realm of God." That is no small order. As Margaret Ann Crain looks for the realm of God in the lives of people she has come to know, Seymour looks for the realm of God in the biblical witness. Both expect God to be revealed. They expect to find God in the experience of human communities, past and present, where God is moving and revealing the potential for New Creation (described often in this book as "realm of God" or "kin-dom of God"). Both also recognize the educative dimensions of redemptive living and the educational potential for building redemptive community. Jack Seymour codifies the educational movements as knowing (paying attention and interpreting); being (developing dispositions of caring); and doing (working to build communities). Education thus has to do with the preparation of whole persons and whole communities to be shaped by God's promise of New Creation. The realm of God is a realm of hope.

The very qualities of knowing, being, and doing characterize the mentees/colleagues of Margaret Ann Crain and Jack Seymour as well. The authors in this volume are activist scholars and scholar activists. They care for the lives of unique persons and unique communities in their diverse academic, ecclesial, and institutional contexts. They also analyze and address social structures, seeking persistently to create a new cultural narrative—a redemptive narrative. Dori Grinenko Baker, Evelyn Parker, Carmichael Crutchfield, and Denise Janssen pay attention to youth and young adults, and to the particularities of their lives, including the lives of incarcerated girls in the case of Parker. Leah Gunning Francis and Reginald Blount pay attention to countercultural narratives and their potential to turn the world upside down. Francis places hope in transformative mentoring, and Blount in freedom schools.

All of these authors—and former students of the dynamic Crain-Seymour duo—recognize the active nature of education. The very process of education depends upon what Débora Junker describes as "embodied redemption." The process does not simply point to redemptive ends, but is itself a redemptive movement. Mai-Anh Le Tran describes the movement in the language of communicability, redeemability, and educability, recognizing that the educational process is a one of opening and receiving new perspectives and new vision. The process involves, as Jack Seymour suggests, a dynamic interplay of knowing, being, and doing. These authors are unanimous in putting forth a bold vision, and in proposing education that is grounded in the practice of paying attention.

Holding Love at the Center

The bold visions of redemptive community arise from the subterranean river of love that flows under and through all of the educational practices described in this book. Dori Grinenko Baker says this simply. In her own educational practice, she attends to "young Moseses and Miriams . . . because I love them . . . " She also wants to "discern future correctives" for the educational communities and practices that sustain these young leaders. The practice of love and the practice of shaping a future are bound together. Redemption flows from love, and love flows from redemption.

The authors here are concerned with brokenness in daily lives and social structures, and they seek to build relationships and redemptive fellowship across time. Leah Gunning Francis attends to relationships of African American women across class divides. For Francis, transformative mentoring involves the same kind of listening and seeing that Crain and Seymour describe. Listening and seeing are acts of love that can be developed through educational processes in order to bring forth and cultivate love in the world. Thus, listening and seeing, both in research and educational practice, are manifestations of love that nurture more love into being.

Trusting God and Choosing Hope

Within the subterranean river of love is a strong current of hope, which marks every chapter in this book. One might see this book as optimistic, but that would be a false reading. This is a book in which the authors face harsh realities and *choose* to hope. Their very choice of religious education as a vocation is an act of hope, namely the hope that what human communities do in their educational actions and structures can make a positive difference in the world. Reginald Blount opens his chapter with an excursus on racism in the United States, and then he defines "the purpose of Christian education to set people free." Carmichael Crutchfield puts forth an educational program called "Enlightened Males," designed to foster full life among African American adolescent boys as they form and transform their identities. Similarly realistic and hopeful in her approach, Débora Junker describes the present moment as "a tumultuous era," but she has high hopes for a path toward redemption, which "should be a path intentionally designed, inviting us to face human contradictions, to confront the prescribed borders that separate us, to contest unfair arrangements, and to expand the possibilities that may lead us in the quest towards transformation." She envisions redemption itself as originating in and contributing to hope: "Redemptive communities are sites of resistance conceived in hope."

The authors of this volume find power to trust God and choose hope as they witness peoples and communities working together for the common good in spite of all odds. They are also motivated by their faith traditions. Not only does Jack Seymour turn to the biblical witness for inspiration, but so do others. Mai-Anh Le Tran, for example, sees reason for hope in the biblical narratives: "Jesus' persistent widow—and, one could say, Jesus himself—reflect tenacious faith in the reparability and redeemability of unjust situations and systems." Evelyn Parker sees the potential of the Bible, and the study of women in the Bible, to help "incarcerated girls identify their bodies as worthy vessels of God."

The authors of this book choose hope in contrast to rose-colored glasses or psychological optimism. Denise Janssen recognizes, for example, how the congregations of young people "let them down at times." Perfection is apparently not the critical factor in the formation of human lives, but hope is vital. Hope is an essential ingredient in the formation both of faith and of resilience; thus, it is central to the design and practice of education in all of its forms. Janssen, speaking of resilient youth, says: "Youth with resilience, driven by hope that frees them from that which threatens to restrain them, find paths and companions and alternate scripts in broken but 'good enough' contexts." Hope thus does not spring from perfection, nor does it lead to perfection, but it provides a "good enough" community to nurture faith and resilience. Hope might be defined in Janssen's words as "paying attention to grace," and opening to and joining in the love that people see all around them.

Appreciating and Cultivating Beauty

The centrality of vision, love, and hope naturally point to the potential of beauty as a mark of redemptive communities. The words creativity, imagination, play, fun, and arts dance throughout this volume, suggesting a strong aesthetic character of education than fosters redemptive community. The very process is aesthetic, beginning with the appreciation of daily life and human lives in diverse, and sometimes threatening, contexts. The process, imbued with the hope described above, aims toward the appreciation of beauty that is already present in a situation and toward the creation or co-creation of more beauty. Mai-Anh Le Tran thus describes education as "artistic work."

The arts and imagination play a major role in education for redemptive community. Débora Junker recognizes the role of poets and prophets in redemptive education. Mai-Anh Le Tran communicates her vision through narratives, and she analyses narratives to discover "the risks and potentialities of human community and human communicability." The narratives reveal how fear, for example, can spread, undercutting the movements of hope. Carmichael Crutchfield, Evelyn Parker, and Denise Janssen similarly communicate through narratives, echoing Jack Seymour's mantra of "paying attention" and Margaret Ann Crain's accent on listening and seeing. These authors also recognize the power of artistic forms to communicate meaning.

In conclusion, the educational movements highlighted in this volume embody vision, love, hope, and art. They do not offer formulas for creating redemptive communities, but they point to God's redemptive movements in creation, and God's invitation to human co-creators who seek to educate for redemptive community in a world that cries out for redemption.

―――― Introduction ――――

Through the Lens of an Ethnographer

Educating for Redemptive Community

―――― *Margaret Ann Crain* ――――

As a RELIGIOUS EDUCATOR with the title *emeritus* I am at the point of asking generative questions. Sometimes I wonder if I wasted all these years as a religious educator. I have tried to empower clergy and laity to be co-creators with God in the redemption of creation. However, I still see a world torn apart by injustice, oppression, and violence. Religion, economics, and politics are flashpoints in conflict. I ask, how have we interfered with God's work in the world and where is the field of religious education in partnership with the *misseo dei*? What has happened to the field of religious education and more specifically, Christian religious education? What new directions must be explored? What old ways must be abandoned in our quest for redemptive community?

Many Christian congregations, particularly of my own denomination, are on hospice care. Have they lost the vision of being a redemptive community? Why? The latest jargon in the church leadership field identifies *the dones,* people who were formerly part of a Christian community but who are now *done* with it and do not expect to ever participate in a church again.[1] Along with the *nones* (people who claim no religious affiliation), the numbers of folks who do not participate in a faith community are growing while church membership is shrinking in the United States. The warning sirens are going off all around us. How did Christian education fail to form disciples who are committed to the fulfillment of the prayer that

1. http://holysoup.com/2014/11/12/the-rise-of-the-dones/ accessed on December 3, 2014.

1

Jesus taught us, "Thy kingdom come. Thy will be done on earth as it is in heaven?"

The church is definitely shrinking, but the jury is out as to the efficacy of religious education. I also see the hopeful signs in congregations that are vital and making a difference in their communities. In some communities people are being formed in ways that empower them to contribute to activities that heal and redeem. In some places the church is more faithful than it has been in a long time.[2] Congregations in the Chicago area are taking a prophetic stand for full inclusion of the LGBTQ community. Other congregations are actively working with immigration issues and helping immigrants to become legal residents of the U.S. Many congregations feed, clothe, and tutor with extravagant generosity. In the fall of 2014, I was especially inspired by the faithful clergy who witnessed to their faith and called for both peace and justice in response to the killing of an unarmed boy in Ferguson, Missouri. The ministries of religious education are key to these vital Christian communities that are making their faith come alive through action.

In addition, the religious educators who are alums of Garrett-Evangelical Theological Seminary keep hope alive. They are a diverse group of people who are living and teaching all around the globe. Former students are now teaching in South Korea, Malaysia, Malawi, Puerto Rico, the Philippines, and all around the United States. They are deeply committed to justice and peace, and they live out those commitments through their teaching and scholarship.

In the fall of 2014, many of these alums returned for an event marking the retirement of Jack L. Seymour entitled *Educating for Redemptive Community*. Conference speakers explored the meaning of *redemptive community* as a commitment that shapes the work of the field of religious education. Seymour's opening lecture quoted Matthew 13:9 where Jesus says, "Pay attention!"[3] Redemptive community is only discovered when we pay attention, whether we are teaching or doing research. Jesus' imperative is the center of my ethnographic approach to research and teaching. Paying attention with an ethnographic lens involves deep listening, careful observation, thick, rich description, and critical analysis. In my opening remarks for the conference, I commented that not only do all of us seek to practice

---

2. Diana Butler Bass paved the way for us to hear this good news in her book, *Christianity for the Rest of Us*. Also see *Greenhouses of Hope* edited by Dori Baker for more stories of congregations that are faithful and prophetic in their youth ministry.

3. *Common English Bible*.

religious education in ways that educate for redemptive community, but we also have experienced a redemptive community[4] at Garrett-Evangelical Theological Seminary as we have learned together. I commented:

> "When we listen to one another expecting to learn and grow, we are embodying redemptive community. When we welcome difference and challenge our own habits and dispositions, we are embodying redemptive community. When we share what we have and rejoice in one another's successes, we are embodying redemptive community."[5]

The three activities named are aspects of redemptive community. They are activities employing an ethnographic lens. In addition, they define the current direction of the field of religious education. Let me discuss each one further.

Living into Redemptive Community

When we listen to one another expecting to learn and grow, we are embodying redemptive community.

For me, listening has become a primary mode of teaching. When we begin to think about pedagogy and classrooms and learners, we now understand that one size does not fit all. Only when each learner is invited to participate with his or her unique needs, interests, and gifts (which have been shaped by family and culture) does genuine learning occur. Learning happens best in a customized context. This can only happen when the learners participate and the teacher listens in order to learn. More and more congregational learning involves small groups where dialogue invites learners to take charge of their own learning and to learn from each other. In my denomination, major investments in a new translation of the Bible and curriculum to accompany it are built around resourcing learners and encouraging them to be in a community of dialogue as they explore what it means to be a disciple of Jesus. Good teachers pay attention.

---

4. I am using the term *redemptive community* loosely here. Essays in this volume will explore the definition more carefully. However, redemptive community should never mean just "nice." This kind of community requires inclusion and justice.

5. Welcome speech by Margaret Ann Crain for "Educating for Redemptive Community," conference held at Garrett-Evangelical Theological Seminary, November 10, 2014.

Even more, listening has become a primary mode of research in the field of religious education. Qualitative research methods such as interviewing and participant observation are revealing new and more complex understandings of how people learn. Scholars are considering the processes of teaching and learning afresh. For far too long teachers focused on the content rather than on the learner. Now we understand that we must engage in deep listening in order to consider the myriad cultural habits, values, and practices that make up human community. They must be taken into account when designing contexts for learning. This is a fundamental shift from the early Twentieth Century when the academic field emerged. Educators began to think about teaching religion, but they were limited by their white, Christian, Western bias. Now we understand that we must abandon the old ways of Christian religious instruction with their Western and white assumptions about human development and learning and instead engage the learners on their own terms.

Since 1988, naturalistic ethnography has been my primary methodological tool for my work in religious education. The processes used in this methodology are deep listening, careful observation, thick rich description, and critical analysis in order to understand what is happening. In a course taught by Professor Yvonna S. Lincoln[6] during my doctoral study, I was converted to naturalistic ethnography as a way of knowing the world. At the time, controversy was still raging among education scholars about the relative value of quantitative and qualitative research methods for evaluating practices in education. Much of education evaluation both then and now depends on standardized tests and other quantitative data to help shape curriculum. Lincoln argued passionately for deep and careful listening and observation as the only way to really understand the complex and multidimensional interactions of teachers and learners. Her commitments were to qualitative research that is naturalistic rather than positivist. Her example of the study of owls illustrated the contrast of the two methodologies: the biologist captures an owl and kills it so that it can be dissected. The bone structure may help to explain how it can fly. The eyes and their connection to the brain may reveal something of its ability to hunt. The contents of the stomach may indicate the diet. This is a more positivist approach with the researcher objectively observing the life of an owl in a

6. Dr. Yvonna S. Lincoln has authored many books about naturalistic qualitative research methods such as *Naturalistic Inquiry* and *Handbook of Qualitative Research*. She is Professor of Higher Education and Educational Administration at Texas A & M University.

disconnected way. The naturalist, on the other hand, may take a chair to the base of the tree where the owl lives and sit quietly, day after day, to observe. After a time, the naturalist becomes part of the forest, and the owl ceases to hide. The owl lives naturally and the researcher watches, until she begins to understand something of the life of an owl. She allows the life of the owl to speak its truths. The naturalistic ethnographer seeks to be in relationship with what she seeks to understand. The relationship respects the other and its life values. The researcher listens and observes in order to describe; the description analyzed leads to understanding.

The naturalistic and ethnographic approach has yielded ever-richer understandings of religious education. Unlike surveys and other quantitative measures, qualitative methods such as interviews and focus groups invite participants to share their own meanings and reveal their hearts and souls as well as their cognitive understandings of faith and discipleship. The essays in this volume are evidence of the rich data that is emerging. Many of these scholars have studied a culture that was home to them. However, like good ethnographers, they have sought to allow the familiar to become strange so that they can see it anew. They describe it and then bring a set of theoretical measures to the data. Often what emerges is a new theory because the old theory does not fit this context. We build on existing knowledge and challenge it with every observation and description.

The naturalistic ethnographic approach is also a part of my teaching practices. I was leading a Bible study recently. The group was diverse. This was the first Bible study for one participant while others were veterans who had read and studied the Bible all throughout their lives. Yet, I was startled when one woman asked the most fundamental question addressed by religious education: "When you use the term *God*, just what do you mean?" Using naturalistic ethnography, I try to listen deeply to this question. I bring to it my knowledge from developmental psychology of how humans mature. I am steeped in the theories of James Fowler, Erik Erikson, Sharon Parks, Carol Gilligan, Mary Field Belenky et. al., and Ruthellen Josselson. I see that some of the women in my group have claimed their own interior authority and are comfortable asking the question about the meaning of the term *God*. Others may have expected me to give an answer to the question based on United Methodist doctrine. They seek an external authority. My own commitments to feminism led me to avoid any gendered pronouns in reference to God, so I had talked about God revealing Godself through the writers of the Bible. Perhaps that language had puzzled the woman and prompted her question. As an ethnographer, I listened to the question. I carefully observed the reactions of the women around the circle even as I analyzed their epistemological viewpoints and thought about how to respond. Creating community is at the center of my pedagogical goals. In fact, that may be my highest goal, rather than to help people learn what the Bible says and means. So, I said to the group, "That is a great question. Let's keep it before us as we read and study the Bible this year." Through my ethnographic lens, I sought to understand what was happening in the mind, heart, and soul of the questioner as I continued to create a community that is a context for learning characterized by justice and respect. In the weekly meetings, we listen to each other, expecting to learn and grow, and in that deep listening we experience redemptive community.

I am still thinking about her question. It points to a post-modern heretical imperative to wonder and to question the pre-modern certainties that much of the church continues to offer. I am convinced that without a community that could hold this woman as she searches for ultimate meanings, she would be a *done*. She would acknowledge that the traditional answers are not congruent with her worldview and fade away from the church.[7]

When we welcome difference and challenge our own habits and dispositions, we are embodying redemptive community.

Not only must we listen, but we must listen also with the expectation that we risk change ourselves. We begin with the acknowledgement that we do not possess all truth; we seek truth together. When we listen with humility, seeking to hear one another and to empower the speaker to share her truth, we have participated in a redemptive community. In order to live into this vision we are pushed to enlarge the voices that are welcome at the table. Religious education must take care to honor the cultural context, the meaningful rituals, the art, the habits and dispositions, the economics, and the power structures in which we live. Religious education must take this entire context into account but not uncritically. We are always holding it up to our understanding of the will of God.

At the same time, we must always be looking critically at our understanding of the will of God. That is why the Bible must be continually reinterpreted and queried with help from the best scholarship. That is why

7. The group did not try to answer the question but acknowledged that it is a question we should keep in mind as we read and study the Bible.

Christian laity must be authorized to think critically. The controversy over sexuality issues in the Christian church in the United States is an example of how our understanding of the will of God keeps shifting and being challenged. About half of the Christians in my denomination are ready to change their traditional definition of marriage and for them it is connected to how they understand God's will for humankind. The other half of us is holding fast to their traditional understanding. They are convinced that sexuality should only be expressed in a marriage between a man and a woman. Both positions claim to be based on biblical authority. We will find our way through this impasse through religious education that studies the Biblical witness in community and continues to reflect together on our understanding of the will of God.

> When we share what we have and rejoice in one another's successes, we are embodying redemptive community.

Learning in community can be risky. In some congregations, a question as fundamental as "What do you mean by God?" is met with shocked silence or an offer to pray for the questioner's lack of faith. Such fundamental questions that are actually relevant or urgent for people are off limits. Learners are forced to maintain a façade of niceness and assent. The Christmas story is a good example of this. Anyone who has learned about the first century knows that miraculous birth stories were told about Caesar and others who needed to seem special. Stories of Jesus' birth found in the gospels attributed to Matthew and Luke are similar to other stories circulating from that time about the births of other special people. We can love the nativity stories as parables that illustrate the special spiritual nature of Jesus. We do not need to put aside our postmodern understandings of the nature of the world to love these stories. Still, many religious education programs in congregations embarrass the questioner or oppress the question entirely.

The growing number of people who identify as *done* with church evidences the risk of community. *The dones* are people who were active in their congregations but claim to be done with the church. Perhaps something happened that alienated them. Perhaps their faith questions were rejected as out of bounds. Or perhaps they have just grown tired of constant requests for more money and time. Perhaps they are weary of the conflict in the community of faith. How is religious education honest about the risk of community? My own experience illustrates the risk and the promise of community. In an eighth grade Sunday School class, I was disgusted when the teacher told us that if even one drop of alcohol ever touched our lips we would end up as bums in the gutter! She was a well-meaning older woman who had been convinced by the WCTU (Women's Christian Temperance Union) that complete abstinence from alcohol was the only safe way to live. I had seen my parents enjoy a drink before dinner and I knew that in moderation alcohol could be enjoyable. As a righteous 13-year-old, I decided that I was never going to attend Sunday School again because it was "dumb." I could easily have become a *done*.

However, the response in this congregation was redemptive. I was invited to become the assistant Sunday School superintendent. I delivered curriculum materials to each class at the beginning of the hour. Then I went back to all the classrooms to collect the offering and attendance records for each class. Finally the superintendent and I tallied the offering and attendance for the day. I felt useful and honored by this task. I worked alongside a faithful young man who treated me like his assistant. My rebellion was accepted and redeemed. I was incorporated back into the community.

The irony is that the girl who hated Sunday School became an ordained religious educator! God must have had a good laugh over that one! The United Methodist Church has been a redemptive community for me. The denomination offered me leadership training, welcomed my leadership, and affirmed and validated my call to ordained ministry. The institution and its practices have nurtured and redeemed me as I have participated in and been educated by its community. At the same time it has broken my heart. It is sometimes oppressive. It uses people and then tosses them aside. It fails to be a force for love, and becomes riddled with judging, hateful, excluding language and rules. While The United Methodist Church can be redemptive, it can also be oppressive.

Community has power to form humans. A student from Malawi described Christian education in his country this way: "People in the community just know that things are right. They learn doctrines through teachers who model through their lives."[8] In the sixteen years that I have been part of the faculty of Garrett-Evangelical Theological Seminary, I have come to see the power of community to educate. What happens in Malawi also can happen in Evanston. When we become part of a community that is redemptive, the educating can move toward the healing of creation and participation in

8. Fletcher Padoko during his qualifying exam at Garrett-Evangelical Theological Seminary, November 12, 2014.

the reign of God. When we participate in a community that is oppressive, we become cynical and bitter and our lives are constrained or we become oppressors. Either way, community is a powerful formative agent for human beings. In order to know the difference, we must pay attention. Deep listening, careful observation, thick rich description, and critical analysis can lead to naming the oppression and moving toward redemptive community. *When we share what we have and rejoice in one another's successes, we are embodying redemptive community.*

As I consider the field of religious education today, I see that it has embraced the imperative to pay attention. We are paying attention to culture, to learners, to the economic and social structures surrounding us, and to our own blindness and entitlements that oppress. I argue that redemptive community is both a research method and the teaching/learning goal. Both are in service of the healing of creation.

Bibliography

Baker, Dori Grinenko, ed. *Greenhouses of Hope: Congregations Growing Young Leaders Who Will Change the World.* Lanham, MD: Rowman & Littlefield, 2010.

Bass, Dorothy Butler. *Christianity for the Rest of Us.* New York: HarperOne, 2006.

The Common English Bible Study Bible with Apocrypha. Nashville: Abingdon, 2013.

Denzin, Norman K. and Yvonna S. Lincoln, eds., *Handbook of Qualitative Research.* Second edition. Los Angeles: Sage, 2000.

http://holysoup.com/2014/11/12/the-rise-of-the-dones/

Lincoln, Yvonna S and Egon G. Guba. *Naturalistic Inquiry,* First Edition. Los Angeles: Sage, 1985.

Pay Attention

Educating for Redemptive Communities

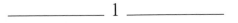 *Jack L. Seymour*

LAST SPRING, AT MY yearly physical, I commented that the office seemed busy. My doctor responded, "That's the new healthcare legislation." "In fact," he added, "I just saw a patient with chronic health issues who hasn't been here in five years. She lost her insurance. While we would have worked with her, she stayed away. Now that she has health insurance again, she is delighted."

He concluded, "The new legislation is a gift. I don't know what you think, but my faith and yours mean we ought to care about and work for others—it is a Mitzvah." You see, he is Jewish and knew I was Christian. I affirmed my ascent. In a few words, we drew deeply on our complementary religious traditions: "Your faith and mine mean we ought to care and work for others—it's a Mitzvah." Our dialogue was a moment of redemptive community, revealing the realm of God. [1]

Defining Redemptive Community

The parable of the sower and soils in the synoptic gospels (and the Gospel of Thomas) points us to abundant grace and redemptive community (Matt 13:3–9; Mark 4:1–9; Luke 4–8; and Thomas: Saying 9). In the parable, Jesus used an ordinary example from the lives of Galileans. A farmer sowed seed for his family. Yet, Jesus' hearers (as too many preachers today) focused

---

1. Sections of this essay were delivered at the November, 2014 Garrett-Evangelical Christian Education Conference. Seeing our PhD and masters' graduates was an honor. Their ministries and scholarship point to redemptive community.

only on the losses in the story: birds that ate the seed, rocks that burned them, and thorns that choked them.

The Galileans knew very well about dead seeds and risky living—that was their life. "Yes," they sighed, "the prophet was right: feeding a family is hard work." To their surprise that was *not* Jesus' point at all. For Jesus, *abundance* was the point. Even with birds, rocks, and thorns, the seeds yielded 30, 60, and 100 fold—(even 120 fold in the Gospel of Thomas)—because of God's redemptive grace.

What? The people were confused and the disciples startled. Seeing their faces, Jesus simply said: "Pay attention (Matt 13:9)."[2] They expected loss; Jesus instead, expected grace.

"Pay attention." How many times in the gospels does Jesus use images of hearing and seeing? Luke's version of this story is a wonderful irony. Jesus tells the disciples, "You have been given the mysteries of God's kingdom (Luke 8:10)." Yet, they do not understand and the parable has to be dissected. The author of Matthew even makes their lack of understanding so ridiculous as to be almost funny. Jesus says: "Happy are your eyes because they see. Happy are your ears because they hear (Matt 13:16)." And the disciples stand dull-witted and baffled.

To make sense of their bafflement, the author of Matthew paraphrases Isaiah (6:9–10), with a twist. (Or was it really Jesus who paraphrased Isaiah?)

> You will hear, to be sure, but never understand;
>
> and you will certainly see but never recognize what you are seeing.
>
> For this people's senses have become calloused,
>
> and they've become hard of hearing,
>
> and they've shut their eyes (Matt 13:14–15).

The people lost their sight and hearing because their senses had become blocked – "had become calloused."

Jesus is very clear that the Galileans (and the disciples) do not see what is in front of them – the realm of God or the redemption of God that is making things new. We can make a list:

- People don't recognize the prophecy of John the Baptist (Matt 11:7–14);

---

2. Unless otherwise noted, all biblical quotations in this chapter are taken from the *Common English Bible* (CEB).

- People of Chorazin, Bethsaida, and Capernaum don't accept the miracles performed in their midst (Matt 11:20–21);
- The disciples refuse to believe that crowds can be fed (Mark 8:9 & Matt 14:21);
- Wedding guests refuse to accept that there will be enough wine (John 2:1–10).

Why were the people unable to see what was in their midst. What blocked them?

We know the world of Roman oppression was difficult:

- The fish of Galilee were harvested and dried to feed soldiers throughout the Empire;
- Hard-working Galileans regularly lost their lands because of debts;
- Wealthy citizens of Jerusalem made profits turning these farms into vineyards and plantations that sold olive oil and wine to the Roman military;
- Illness and demon possession spread as a result of poverty and abuse; and
- The people were rightfully afraid.

Seeking to protect themselves, people withdrew and hid and hoarded what little they had. Fear and its results hardened their senses. They were numbed.

Yet, throughout the reports of the gospels, Jesus argued that there was another way other than fear and withdrawal to address these ongoing crises—for the realm of God was present in redemptive communities. Jesus did not deny oppression, nor its harshness. He pleaded to God:

- Bring in your kingdom so that your will is done on earth as it's done in heaven (Matt 6:10).
- Give us the bread we need for today (Matt 6:11).
- Do not bring us to the time of trial (Luke 11:4 NRSV).

Yet, as he prayed for new life, he simultaneously witnessed that care and hope were already present in acts of redemptive community, saying, "Your heavenly Father knows that you need them (Matt 6:32)." For Jesus, God's grace was abundant. Hungry were being fed; thirsty given drink; strangers welcomed; and imprisoned visited and freed (see Matt 25:31–46).

Going deeper, look at that last comment: the imprisoned were visited and freed. Why were people imprisoned in Jesus' day? Of course, there were petty thieves. Yet, most imprisonment resulted from acts the Romans considered as rebellion – from outright insurrection to not paying debts, or theft, or even demon possession. When Jesus said that prisoners were freed, he was not talking about "jail breaks." Rather, he focused on profound acts of restoring people to community.

In fact, all of the claims he made about his work were directly about restoring community. Healing and freeing brings people back into community. That's the good news. Even in the midst of oppression, the realm of God is possible. Redemptive community can be built, if we stop hoarding, hiding, and excluding. Even senses can be freed from the results of abuse. Interestingly, the words of Jesus confront both the powerful and weak— both with the message of redemptive community.

I believe this "economic" reading of Jesus' kingdom sayings is confirmed by the actions of the early Christian community as they spread throughout the world. As they gathered for study and worship, they shared community and their wealth. They raised collections for the poor and sent food from their tables to those in need. Furthermore, in Rome, many lived in common tenement buildings and ate and prayed together at day's end, after a day's labor. Even the wealthier in their midst paid for the food for their communion celebrations.

They continued the ministries Jesus expected of his disciples—healing, freedom, and proclamation. Sociologist, Rodney Stark, has described well that first Christian community:

> The Church didn't clean up the streets. Christians didn't put in sewers. So you still had to live with a trench running down the middle of the road, in which you could find dead bodies decomposing. But what Christians did was take care of each other. Their apartments were as smoky as the pagan apartments, since neither had chimneys, and they were cold and wet and they stank. But Christians loved one another, and when they got sick they took care of each other. Someone brought you soup. You can do an enormous amount to relieve those miseries if you look after each other.[3]

3. "A Double Take on Early Christianity: An Interview with Rodney Stark" in http://www.jknirp.com/stark.htm. These values were true for both Jewish and Christian communities. See Stark, *The Rise of Christianity*.

In a time of risk, poverty, and oppression, people prayed for relief, they hoped for the realm of God, but they continued to offer each other sustenance as they challenged powers and principalities. Stark even argues health and healthcare were better in Jewish and Christian communities because of faith.

What does redemptive community mean? Pay attention to the signs of the realm of God in your midst. Invite strangers, eat with the outcasts, make friends with tax collectors, and set banquet tables. All these were among Jesus' invitations. Specifically, pray for relief; challenge the principalities and powers that feed fear and callousness; and work for community.[4]

In other words, rebuilding community offers life! Or, as the New Testament scholar, Jose Pagolo, has summarized: healing, defending the poor, demanding justice, and offering forgiveness are evidences of God's saving community.

> The purpose of the gospels is to reveal the saving presence of God, who raised Jesus but who was acting in his life even before that. When Jesus healed the sick, he was conveying to them the power, the health, and the life of the same God who has now revealed all his saving power by raising Jesus from death. When he defended the poor, victims of so much injustice, he was demanding the justice of the same God who defended him by raising him from among the dead. When he accepted 'sinners and tax collectors' at his table, he was offering them the same forgiveness and peace of God that the disciples are now enjoying in the presence of the Risen One.[5]

Understanding Redemptive Community Today

Turning this analysis to today, remember my doctor's comments: "Your faith and mine mean we ought to care and work for others—it's a Mitzvah." What are the realities of economic life to which he pointed me? Clearly, he was commenting on the extension of healthcare and the political firestorm that still surrounds it. More than that, we know the middle class is shrinking as the gap of wealth and poverty increases. In addition, some politicians

---

4. For a fuller development of this idea, see chapter 7 in my *Teaching the Way of Jesus*.

5. Pagolo, *Jesus: An Historical Approximation*, 417.

use scare tactics about balanced budgets to systematically destroy the economic safety net.[6]

Rising inequality may be, as President Obama has suggested, the "defining challenge of our time." Inequality has resulted in "rapidly growing deficit of opportunity."[7] Economists Emmanuel Saez and Gabriel Zucman note that gap is increasing:

> The rise of wealth inequality is almost entirely due to the rise of the top 0.1 percent wealth share, from 7 percent in 1979 to 22 percent in 2012—a level almost as high as in 1929. The bottom 90 percent wealth share first increased up to the mid-1980s and then steadily declined. The increase in wealth concentration is due to the surge of top incomes combined with an increase in saving rate inequality. Top wealth-holders are younger today than in the 1960s and earn a higher fraction of total labor income in the economy.[8]

What are the consequences of this reality? Many social problems can be traced directly to inequality—poor educational attainment, poor health, increasingly inadequate neighborhoods, limiting of resources for schools and pre-schools, and crime. For example, the children of the advantaged progress faster as the poor start further behind.[9] Addressing the growing wealth/income inequality is crucial for a healthy future and a thriving national community.

A recent Pew Research Global Attitudes Report discovered too many people blame inequality on the "laziness" of the poor. They think that gaps

6. I thank economist Greg Seymour for helping me understand the impact of these arguments. See Piketty, *Capital in the 21st Century*, and Stiglitz and Greenwald, *Creating a Learning Society: A New Approach to Growth, Development, and Social Progress*.

7. President Obama in a speech given before the Center for American Progress on December 4, 2013. See http://www.pbs.org/newshour/rundown/obama-set-to-speak-on-income-gap-between-rich-and-poor/. See also Emily Badger's summary of a report on the economic consequences of inequality, by Manuel Pastor, the director of the Program for Environmental and Regional Equity at USC. http://www.washingtonpost.com/blogs/wonkblog/wp/2014/10/28/what-the-u-s-economy-would-look-like-if-racial-inequality-didnt-exist/

8. Saez and Zucman, "Wealth Inequality in the United States since 1913," 1.

9. See O'Brien, "Poor kids who do everything right don't do better than rich kids who do everything wrong," http://www.washingtonpost.com/blogs/wonkblog/wp/2014/10/18/poor-kids-who-do-everything-right-dont-do-better-than-rich-kids-who-do-everything-wrong/.

of opportunity are caused by a lack of responsibility. They ignore how inequality perpetuates inequality, as well as fear and despair.[10]

Why do ideas such as "promoting responsibility" and "developing a caring safety net" have to be seen as polar opposites used to relieve us of our responsibilities to community? Can't we advocate for both building responsibility and furthering economic opportunity? A personal example: My aunt worked 40 years in an automobile factory regularly putting aside money for retirement, paying health insurance, and adding additional retirement insurance. She was always healthy and active. After she retired she contracted a virulent disease that left her in isolation and confusion. All of her savings and insurance were not enough for the financial onslaught of hospitalization and nursing home care—in fact many times the savings of a fragile life. Losing everything and going on Medicaid was the only way she could endure—and then, with the help of family, only in risky fashion. She needed a *Mitzvah*.

Don't we have a "collective responsibility to people in need?"[11] How can any religious person participate in the deceptive practices that fuel inequality and deny a safety net to those with whom we share life and community? Too often many simply do not believe in giving a *Mitzvah*.

Educating for redemptive community means learning to *pay attention*, or, as noted above, praying for relief, challenging principalities and powers, and working for community. Paying attention is a form of interpretation—looking for and following the realm of God. We see ways our lives can be transformed. We join in the actions and ministries to which Jesus called us—to rebuild communities.

The Quandary: Education and Redemptive Community

Here is a practical quandary with which we must deal as religious educators. Jesus' contemporaries in Galilee had a rich educative environment. Why with quality education, did Jesus have to shout, "Pay attention?" Why were some blocked from experiencing the empowerment offered by God's

---

10. See http://www.pewglobal.org/2014/10/09/emerging-and-developing-economies-much-more-optimistic-than-rich-countries-about-the-future/

11. This phrase was used by Doris Kearns Goodwin in describing the call of Franklin Roosevelt for a more active role for government. From Ken Burns, *The Roosevelts: An Intimate History*, Episode 6: "The Common Cause." *http://www.pbs.org/kenburns/the-roosevelts/*

abundant grace? We have already seen the answer: fear and despair had so much power.

Remember the fullness of the education that Jesus and others had: It began with the daily reminder in the *Shema*, prayed every morning and evening, to love God and neighbor. Each week, each Sabbath in home and community, the prayers of the people focused their total dependence upon God. Moreover, through prescribed great festivals like *Pesach*, *Shavuot*, *Sukkoth*, *Rosh Hashanah* and *Yom Kippur*, the people learned that freedom was God's gift; that the covenant was God's initiation; that God was a protector and nurturer; and that new life was possible. Indeed, this was a rich set of educational practices.

Therefore, why did even disciples have trouble hearing and seeing? Of course, some of it was due to the same realities we face today of people hearing only part of what is proclaimed or of only committing part of their lives. In addition, clearly some of it was due to a lack of moral integrity. As everywhere, some took advantage of the Roman power structure and benefitted from it. That is clearly not the case for most. Reform movements, like the Pharisees, worked to extend faithfulness to *all* moments of living. That was the meaning of the oral *Torah*. They argued with the Sadducees and those in power that the expectations of the *Torah* claimed people in new ways and in new times. In addition, both the deeply religious faithful across Galilee and some of the apocalyptic parties, like the John the Baptizer group, regularly reinforced the expectations of loving God and neighbors.

Why gaps of understanding? Remember all teaching occurs in the midst of a social context. The realities of people's lives profoundly affect the ways they hear teaching, receive it, and engage it. To understand the gaps, we need to look to the social situation itself, the situation of oppression and advantage for many poor and wealthy alike that resulted in a failure of the senses.[12] Had some given up on the hope built into the festivals, did some ignore the responsibilities embedded in them, did others focus only on surviving the everyday, and did still others close their eyes as they sought to hold off further onslaught from the Romans? We know that depression and despair consumes energy, insight, and action.

The economic analysis of Galilee and Palestine in Roman times suggests that there was contempt between those living in Jerusalem and "country peasants." Moreover, people were divided into two major classes: the elites that made up one percent of the population, and the peasants.

12. Schwartz, *Imperialism and Jewish Society*.

In terms of power and wealth, the differences between these groups were significant.[13] Moreover, the elites connected with the military and political leadership. Therefore, the elites were protected as the ordinary people, in turn, found themselves dependent.

The majority of rural "peasants" (90 percent of the people) consisted of small landholders who sought to provide for families, tenant farmers, day laborers and slaves. In the small villages and towns of the region as well as the cities like Sepphoris and Tiberius were merchants, artisans, and workers of various kinds—all dependent on the wants of the wealthy and on public works projects, e.g. the rebuilding of Sepphoris. At the base, were a large group of unclean and dismissed peoples from bandits to prostitutes to lepers.[14]

While many people earned just enough to feed families and get by, the wealth gap was immense. For most, daily life was at risk of storm, natural disaster, war, insurrections (as had occurred in Sepphoris at time of Herod the Great), theft, or increased taxation (until the mid-40s CE, Rome gave the Herodian family much freedom to tax the region of Galilee). Life was on the edge. The social safety net was negligible. Increasingly as indebtedness grew and lands sold, wealthy persons in Judea bought up parcels and wove them together into estates and vineyards marketing to Roman authorities.[15] People were consumed, as is true in most times, with the daily activities of getting by—of raising children, of feeding families, of seeking employment, and of protecting what little they had.

In contrast, what did Jesus do and proclaim? As we have seen, he prayed for God's guidance, he reminded people of their great traditions of loving God and neighbor, and he healed and freed where he could. In other words, he promoted communities of care. He knew that only when the vulnerable are surrounded with care and support are they able to survive. As prophets before, he was particularly critical of aristocrats who built their fortunes on others. Moreover, he expected followers to live so that caring made a significant difference—sending them to heal, forgive, and witness. In small and personal ways, they offered new life. Yet that experience of new life opened up even grander hopes for community.

---

13. See Fiensy, *Christian Origins and the Ancient Economy*, 9, 35.

14. Fiensy, *Christian Origins*, 14–35. See also Malina, *The Social World of Jesus and the Gospels*.

15. See Schwartz, *Imperialism and Jewish Society*.

In a town like Capernaum, where a community of artisans and fisherman gathered around him, the realities of redemptive community could be experienced. The same is true in the early communities discussed in Acts and those we know that existed later in Rome. The social safety net demanded by the Jewish tradition and upheld in Jesus' vision of the kingdom empowered people to heal, visit, care for, free, distribute food, collect money, and even pay the bond for indentured servants.[16] In the midst of immense gaps of wealth and power, Jesus encouraged people to do what they could to make life different and witness to God's abundant grace.

Context profoundly affects what is learned. Educating for redemptive community is not easy. To Jesus the signs of redemptive community were obvious and they demanded response. He called for people to pay attention. Many were simply too depressed and abused to see it. Others saw glimpses of new life and community in healings, in forgiveness, and in restored communities. Those glimpses encouraged them to reach out to others—to seek new options.

Isn't this true for us too? What affects our senses? Are we sometimes calloused, broken, simply living, or simply getting ahead? Many of the same reasons that blocked people in Jesus' day may be blocking us today.

Educating for Redemptive Community

Here then is the challenge: we faithfully educate when we help people pay attention and follow God's vision for redemption. Clearly, having a rich educative environment is not enough. Religious education must therefore be focused and explicit enough to address and break through everyday realities and expectations.[17] We educate for redemptive community at the same time as we work to build it—to make it a reality in people's lives. Experiencing a glimpse of redemptive community empowers us to work even harder to expand it.

---

16. For a fuller description of the actions of the early Christian community, see Stark, *The Rise of Christianity*.

17. This is the hard work that many graduates of the Garrett-Evangelical Theological Seminary PhD program in Christian education and congregational studies are engaged. They offer hope by enlivening children and youth ministries; recovering culturally-embodied theologies and practices; connecting theological education to social justice; stimulating moral education; enhancing teaching practices; strengthening spiritual formation; and expanding faithful leadership.

Let me offer three suggestions about how we might be focused and explicit—enhancing education for redemptive community. I think these are present in the education that Jesus led. I believe it is our responsibility to continue them as we seek to affect congregational, public, and theological life.

1. Knowing—Immersing People in God's Vision of Redemptive Community

Education always points us in a direction. Education teaches us to pay attention. A parent explicitly teaches values to a child and works so the child will live out those values. Music teachers explicitly teach skills and techniques to pupils so that they grow as musicians. Theological educators teach students how to draw on the resources of the faith to empower their ministry. All education points us in a direction.

Therefore, as we know, all education is political. Education shapes the future—the ways people think, feel and act. Acknowledging this political reality, we need to decide explicitly what we will teach, how we will teach it, and how we seek to affect the future. In fact, Lawrence Cremin, former president of Teacher's College, has written that the task of all good education is prophecy—or calling a people back to their deepest and most important commitments.[18]

Faithful education is explicit and focused. We have limited time and the people with whom we work have limited patience. As we have seen, even a rich "general" religious education is not enough, particularly when a context of fear is present. With passion, we need to point to and invite people into a *particular* vision—that of God's realm of abundant grace. That is what Jesus did. He reminded the people of their traditions and social situation, but even more than that he pointed to new possibilities. He demonstrated that people could indeed live redemptively, even in small ways—that living could be different.

Our task is to point directly to God's vision of redemptive community, so people can see new possibilities. Nothing is more important! We humans are notoriously forgetful. We miss the important as we obsess on the obvious—whether it is caused by fear, everydayness, or brokenness. In response, we are working to help people acquire a new vocabulary to interpret their lives in light of a new reality.

18. Cremin, *Public Education.*

As I write these words, important protests are occurring throughout the U.S. reminding all that "Black Lives Matter." The realities of violence, to which they point, make apparent that economic and political exploitation have not changed for many persons of color. Through the protests, the public is reminded that God created all as children of God—all matter. Theological and religious education are key public partners in calling for an inclusive community where all thrive.[19]

Therefore education for redemption is a form of knowing—of interpretation. Redemption is a way of looking at our world and its possibilities, and engaging them. Through the eyes of redemptive existence, we learn to interpret the realities of our contexts differently. We see what we missed before. As theologian, Edward Farley, argues:

> [W]hat God does to save is to found a community of redemption ... Bound in close relationships with other human beings who are responding to the gospel narrative, human beings experience new freedoms in their ways of being, thinking, and feeling, and in their relationships.... The symbolism and the story of redemption reach the depths of individuals as they interpret and reinterpret themselves and their world. Redemption can liberate the human being from every level of human evil: systematic oppression, skewed personal relationships, and the loss of individual freedom."[20]

To educate for redemption thus means to keep in front of people God's vision. To then ask, over and over: how we are living it?

In fact, theologically, "redemptive community" redefines what we mean when we use the word salvation or say "Jesus Saves."[21] Saving includes all of the acts of the realm of God to which Jesus pointed. "Jesus saves" when we engage in:

- Healing the sick,

- Giving sight to the blind,

19. For example, the 2014 meeting of the Religious Education Association focused on "Religion and Education in the (Un)making of Violence" explicitly attended to ongoing racism and proposing explicit strategies for education. Thanks for the leadership of Mai-Anh Le Tran of Eden Seminary. See also Leah Gunning Francis, "A Boy, a Wrestler and the Racialized Imagination," in *Race Matters in the Classroom*, a blog of the Wabash Center for Teaching and Learning in Theology and Religion. http://wabashcenter.typepad.com/antiracism_pedagogy/

20. Farley, *Practicing Gospel*, 5–6.

21. I thank Charles Foster for this insight that our definitions of salvation block us or open us to see or hear new possibilities.

- Offering hearing to those who are deaf,
- Forgiving those who have sinned,
- Proclaiming release to prisoners,
- Preaching the good news to the poor, the least of these,
- Restoring community, and
- Enacting Shalom.[22]

2. Being—Developing Dispositions of Caring

Knowing, however, is not enough. Unless focusing on and caring for the other become fundamental aspects of our beings, nothing will change. We will talk a good story, but not live it. Like the early Christian community, we need a conversion to the other.[23]

Recently, I heard two five-year old boys talking at a playground. For a moment, their conversation embodied caring. One boy said, "Let's play." His new acquaintance responded, "What?" The first said, "How about army? We could shoot bad guys." To which the second ended their talk, "I don't want to play that." The first: "What then do you want to play?" The second: "I want to play better games."

When speaking with the second boys' mother, she told me that his pre-school explicitly teaches the children what are good games and games that hurt. They want to develop a disposition of non-violent play in children. He has learned his school's language well. He was practicing it when he said, "I want to play better games."

How do we shape the dispositions of our children, of ourselves, so we "play" better games? The prophet Micah offers a direction. Remember his message:

---

22. See my *Teaching the Way of Jesus*, 132–133. These markers come from an analysis of Jesus' sermon in Nazareth Luke 4:16–30), at his response to John's disciples (Matt 11:2–6), and at his sending his disciples into ministry (Matt 10:5–8).

23. Dori Baker and Reggie Blount have demonstrated through their work on vocation that lives can be formed that are empowered and focused on caring and the other. See Baker and Mercer, *Lives to Offer*, and Baker's blog at fteleaders.org. See also Reginald Blount, "In Search of Living Waters: The Seven Spiritual Yearnings of Youth" at https://www.ptsem.edu/uploadedFiles/School_of_Christian_Vocation_and_Mission/Institute_for_Youth_Ministry/Princeton_Lectures/Blount-Search.pdf.

> [God] has told you, human one, what is good and what the Lord requires from you: to do justice, *embrace faithful love*, and walk humbly with your God (Mic 6:8).

"Embrace faithful love" is a translation of the concept *hesed*. Fundamentally, *hesed* is about God's action of covenanting with a people—of loving them so much that they respond, in turn, in love and covenant. In fact, in the third century, Rabbi Simlai, who is thought to have numbered the *Mitzvah* (613 positive and 365 negative), said that this simple verse defines all God's expectations.[24] It is the best reflection of a *Mitzvah*. In her commentary, Katherine Sakenfeld adds that this verse is about developing a *disposition* of the heart where the task of the faithful is " . . . active concern for the well-being of all the people of God, not just those known personally, and particularly [for] the poor!"[25] Developing a disposition is the second task of educating for redemptive community. Education moves from knowing to training the human heart so that we are oriented toward the other.

How do we "train" dispositions? A recent study of 10,000 middle and high school students offers a clue. In *The Parents We Mean to Be*, Harvard psychologist, Richard Weissbourd shares the startling finding that 80 percent of the youth interviewed believed their parents were more concerned about their achievements, rather than whether they learned to "care for others." Weissbourd is clear that we need to counter this self-centeredness. To do so, he has founded a project called "Making Caring Common."

Shaping a disposition of caring is "like learning a sport: repetition helps." He continues: "A good person is something one can always become. . . . Capacities for caring and fairness" can be developed as well as "ethical capacities."[26] Caring and paying attention to the vulnerable can be learned. They are taught by immersion and by practice.

Thinking about educating for caring leads us directly to strategies of learning in doing, in working to build and enhance communities. We learn as we immerse ourselves in activities of caring, empathy, and engagement. We need to study closely and learn from projects like "Making Caring

---

24. Ehud Ben Zvi, "Introductions and Annotations: The Twelve Minor Prophets," 1215.

25. See Sakenfeld, "Love (OT)", 378–380, and Sakenfeld, *The Meaning of Hesed in the Hebrew Bible*.

26. Weissbourd et.al., *The Children We Mean to Raise*. See also *The Christian Century* (August 20, 2014) 8, and the website for the project http://sites.gse.harvard.edu/making-caring-common?keyword=making_caring_common&tabgroupid=icb.tabgroup160892.

Common." They offer us pedagogical practices for shaping dispositions.[27] The second task of educating for redemptive community is directing people's dispositions toward caring.

3. Doing—Working to Build Communities

In a recent interview for the Youth Ministry Initiative sponsored by Yale University School of Theology, Dr. Evelyn Parker defined ways to help youth confront racial injustice. She argued that faithful youth ministry taught concrete *practices (actions)*: to recognize racism, ritualize and lament it, resist it directly, and seek reconciliation both within and without. The goal of these practices is redemption or "living wholesome lives." To her, redemption is actively resisting "the status quo to create something new so all can thrive."[28]

Redemptive action offers alternatives to powers and principalities. Or, as we saw in the ministry of Jesus, he prayed for relief, challenged powers that fed fear, and worked for community by healing, freeing, and inviting people into new life. We know that his actions did not transform the whole social structure of Roman oppression, nor did they counter all of the despair and brokenness it caused. Rather, they offered glimpses and moments of genuine redemptive community. His work gave people experience with new life and pointed to promises of transformed living.

Therefore, as educators, we need to attend to concrete practical ways to build community and offer redemption. We learn in the midst of doing. While our actions may resist powers and principalities, more likely they will be local and limited. Yet, they are real moments of new life. As we know, new life gives birth to more new life. These actions witness that we can indeed make a profound difference in peoples' ways of living.

To understand the meaning of witness, I turn to the Jewish philosopher Peter Ochs. He speaks of the need for "small acts" that stand against terror.[29] These small acts are real moments of new life that "witness" and

---

27 Other projects include "Roots of Empathy" (www.rootsofempathy.org) for building "caring, peaceful and civil societies," or the Children's Defense Fund—to "ensure every child a Healthy Start, a Head Start, a Fair Start, a Safe Start and a Moral Start in life"(www.childrensdefense.org)."

28. See Evelyn Parker at the Yale Youth Ministry Initiative when she speaks about redemption: http://www.youtube.com/watch?v=MhWzv8rb9Ow.

29. Peter Ochs, "Small Actions Against Terror," 287–304.

demonstrate that life can be different—communities of care can be built. For Ochs, the notion of "small acts" was a response to the power of immense and systemic evil embodied in the Holocaust. Of course, structural efforts of resistance and challenge are also essential, but these usually begin as small, local acts. The very existence of "small acts" offers options and demonstrates possibilities.

People of goodwill can stand together, engaging in small acts of justice that make a difference where they are—embodying redemptive community. The power of the Roman Empire and its complicitors were also evil. Here many, including Jesus and his followers, as well as many of his Jewish and Gentile contemporaries began with small acts—acts of healing, visiting prisoners, forgiving, and restoring people to communities. These acts were moments of light in the darkness; moments that can spread and multiply.

As educators, we encourage both protest and resistance against powers and principalities as well as small acts of building community. We help people see possibilities by assisting them to name concerns to be addressed, analyze effective ways to engage these issues, and develop concrete strategies to act. One way this process of teaching has been described is as "see-judge-act."[30] Education and community organization are united. Education begins by helping people see, to name the powers and principalities that oppress, misguide, or limit. Analysis and critique follow as problems are defined and options explored. Finally, action occurs as people seek to build communities—to join in coalitions to extend healing, support, and care. We engage intentional projects to address the common good.

Therefore, people learn about redemptive community as they participate in seeking to make it a reality. Their work is like that of sustaining an NGO or a social justice agency—building relationships, inviting coalitions, writing grants, speaking with strangers, and organizing groups to work to make life better.

Focused on the vision of the realm of God and supported by a deep spirituality of living God's realm, we engage in action for the common good. As we do we are engaged in a dynamic process of doing, reflecting, and doing again. Knowing, being, and doing coalesce.

---

30. *The National Plan for Hispanic/Latino Ministry of The United Methodist Church, 2013-2016 Quadrennium Booklet,* 8. The notion, see-judge-act was first used in the Catholic Workers Movement, see the website of the Young Christian Workers, http://www.cijoc.org/ where these skills are described as well as ways to teach them.

Living Toward Redemptive Community

Jesus told the disciples and those who heard him, "Pay attention." We repeat that today. We need a particular kind of religious education, an education that explicitly seeks to redeem the contexts in which learning takes place and purposefully focuses on teaching and building redemptive community.

Just as in Jesus' day, principalities of power and wealth divide and mislead. The growing gap of wealth results in a growing gap of inequality and opportunity. People despair and are blinded to options. They are numbed and misguided by those who tell them that balanced budgets are more important than safety nets, excellent schools, thriving neighborhoods, and extending healthcare. While fiscal responsibility is an important goal, it must be coupled with efforts to build communities of hope, justice, and thriving. As Richard Weissbourd of "Making Caring Common" says, "Any healthy civil society also depends on adults who are committed to their communities and who, at pivotal times, will put the common good before their own."[31] Preparing persons who care about the common good and work together to shape it is our civic and religious responsibility.

Our task, guided by the marks of salvation to which Jesus pointed, is to teach the vision of redemptive community, work to help people develop dispositions of care for others, and act, even in small ways, that make a difference. Teaching redemptive community means calling people to actions that

- Heal the sick,
- Give sight to the blind,
- Offer hearing to those who are deaf,
- Forgive those who have sinned,
- Proclaim release to prisoners,
- Offer good news to the poor, the least of these,
- Restore community, and
- Enact Shalom.[32]

31. Executive Summary, *Making Caring Common*. *http://isites.harvard.edu/fs/docs/ icb.topic1430903.files//Executive%20Summary.pdf.*

32. See my *Teaching the Way of Jesus*, 132–133. These markers come from an analysis of Jesus' sermon in Nazareth (Luke 4:16–30), at his response to John's disciples (Matt 11:2–6), and at his sending his disciples into ministry (Matt 10:5–8).

Whenever we do these things, we are living out our religious responsibilities in a way that has a public impact. Or, to use the words of Fr. Pagolo, we follow Jesus:

> "Jesus launched a movement of followers to proclaim and promote his plan for the reign of God . . . . What could be more important for followers of Jesus in our time, than committing ourselves to a true conversion of Christianity to the reign of God."[33]

That is what we mean by educating for and living for redemptive community. Pay attention:

- Be immersed in the vision of the redemptive community—know it.
- Work to develop dispositions of care—be redemptive.
- Engage and learn the concrete strategies of resistance and of justice—do and live for justice and new life.

Bibliography

Baker, Dori Grinenko and Joyce Mercer. *Lives to Offer: Accompanying Youth on Their Vocational Quests.* Cleveland: Pilgrim, 2007.

Blount, Reginald. "In Search of Living Waters: The Seven Spiritual Yearnings of Youth." https://www.ptsem.edu/uploadedFiles/School_of_Christian_Vocation_and_Mission/Institute_for_Youth_Ministry/Princeton_Lectures/Blount-Search.pdf.

Burns, Ken. *The Roosevelts: An Intimate History,* Episode 6: "The Common Cause." http://www.pbs.org/kenburns/the-roosevelts/

Common English Bible. Nashville: Abingdon, 2013.

Cremin, Lawrence. *Public Education.* New York: Basic Books, 1990.

"A Double Take on Early Christianity: An Interview with Rodney Stark" in http://www.jknirp.com/stark.htm.

Farley, Edward. *Practicing Gospel: Unconventional Thoughts on the Church's Ministry.* Louisville: Westminster John Knox, 2003.

Fiensy, David. *Christian Origins and the Ancient Economy.* Cambridge, MA: James Clarke & Co., 2014.

Francis, Leah Gunning. "A Boy, a Wrestler and the Racialized Imagination," in *Race Matters in the Classroom,* a blog of the Wabash Center for Teaching and Learning in Theology and Religion. http://wabashcenter.typepad.com/antiracism_pedagogy/

Malina, Bruce. *The Social World of Jesus and the Gospels.* London: Routledge, 1996.

The National Plan for Hispanic/Latino Ministry of The United Methodist Church, 2013-2016 Quadrennium Booklet. New York: National Plan for Hispanic/Latino Ministry, 2013.

33. Pagolo, *Jesus: An Historical Approximation,* 448.

O'Brien, Matt. "Poor kids who do everything right don't do better than rich kids who do everything wrong." *The Washington Post.* http://www.washingtonpost.com/blogs/wonkblog/wp/2014/10/18/poor-kids-who-do-everything-right-dont-do-better-than-rich-kids-who-do-everything-wrong/

Ochs, Peter. "Small Actions Against Terror: Jewish Reflections on a Christian Witness," in *Against Terror: A Witness to Love and Justice.* Victoria Erickson, ed. Ada, MI: Brazos, 2001.

Pagolo, Jose. *Jesus: An Historical Approximation,* Rev. ed. Miami: Convivium, 2012.

Parker, Evelyn. http://www.youtube.com/watch?v=MhWzv8rb9Ow.

Piketty, Thomas. *Capital in the 21st Century.* Cambridge, MA: Harvard University Press, 2014.

Saez, Emmanuel and Gabriel Zucman. "Wealth Inequality in the United States since 1913: Evidence from Capitalized Income Tax Data," *Working Paper 20625,* (National Bureau of Economic Research, October 2014) 1. http://www.nber.org/papers/w20625

Sakenfeld, Katharine Doob. "Love (OT)" in *Anchor Bible Dictionary.* David Noel Freedman, ed. New York: Doubleday, 1992. IV 378–380

Sakenfeld, Katherine Doob. *The Meaning of Hesed in the Hebrew Bible: A New Inquiry.* Wipf & Stock, 2002.

Schwartz, Seth. *Imperialism and Jewish Society: 200 BCE to 640 CE.* Princeton, NJ: Princeton University Press, 2004.

Seymour, Jack L. *Teaching the Way of Jesus: Educating Christians for Faithful Living.* Nashville: Abingdon, 2014.

Stark, Rodney. *The Rise of Christianity: How an Obscure, Marginal Jesus Movement Became the Dominant Religious Force in the Western World in a Few Centuries.* San Francisco: HarperSanFrancisco, 1997.

Stiglitz, Joseph E. and Bruce C. Greenwald, *Creating a Learning Society: A New Approach to Growth, Development, and Social Progress.* New York: Columbia University Press, 2014.

Weissbourd, Richard. Executive Summary, *Making Caring Common. http://isites.harvard.edu/fs/docs/icb.topic1430903.files//Executive%20Summary.pdf.*

Weissbourd, Rick and Stephanie Jones, with Trisha Ross Anderson, Jennifer Kahn, Mark Russell. *The Children We Mean to Raise: The Real Message Adults are Sending about Values.* Cambridge, MA: Harvard Graduate School of Education, 2014.

Zvi, Ehud Ben. "Introductions and Annotations: The Twelve Minor Prophets," *The Jewish Study Bible.* Adele Berlin and Marc Zvi Brettler, eds. New York: Oxford University Press, 2004

———————— 2 ————————

Moseses, Miriams, and
Monarch Migrations

Teaching for Redemptive Community

———— *Dori Grinenko Baker* ————

I BELIEVE THERE IS a future wanting to emerge through progressive religious leaders who desire the healing of the earth and its people. I invest my time helping to nurture young adult leaders who want to be part of that future. Redemptive community emerges from inviting the unleashing of hope and possibility in those with whom we work. It means following the spirit of God enlivening the fragile elements in creation.

In this essay, I will make three moves:

1. I will begin with an auto-ethnographic definition of our theme. I hope to show that educating for redemptive community is present in the concrete realities of daily life.

2. I will share some ethnographic observations from my perch as a listener to a cohort of young Americans who identify as followers of God and followers of Jesus.

3. Finally, I will invite us to wonder together about the future of our collective work as religious educators in an era of "principled pluralism."

In these comments, I am hopeful. There are many sources for this hopefulness—on my good days.

Yet, I must admit that the work of religious leadership is arduous—*bad days do dawn*. Those hard days are made bearable and often surprisingly gratifying because of friends who accompany us on our winding, varied, and quirky vocational journeys. My reflections here join a larger chorus. I hope you, reader, find a measure of companionship as you enter this conversation. You are not alone.

For me, religious education is a vocation in which I find meaning and purpose. I think of myself as a contemplative activist/scholar working *within* the Christian tradition, while always focusing an interested and collaborative spirit toward fellow travelers in other faith traditions. I maintain this stance in part by holding fast to three affirmations that Jack Seymour and others have taught me through their teaching, writing and living.

1. As theologians and meaning-makers, religious educators are always about the work of helping others become the theologians and meaning makers of their own life experiences.

2. Our meaning making takes place at the very innermost core of our individual beings, and simultaneously and necessarily at the outer edge of our traditions, where it must do the risky work of ongoing public interpretation if it is to be redemptive.

3. Our meaning making is not for the sake of inner peace, nor for the sake of preserving our traditions or institutions—although these are surely sacred purposes—but always for the sake of an aching world and ever-expanding notions of "who is my neighbor" *now* and who might be *becoming* my neighbor in the near or distant future.

These three commitments emerged in my practice and scholarship as I moved from graduate school, where Jack Seymour served as a dissertation adviser, into a career as an independent scholar, writer, and college chaplain. I offer them here as a starting point to give flesh to what "educating for redemptive community" looks like from my context, where I focus on leadership development with young adults.

After a deep immersion into the worlds of these young adult Moseses and Miriams I encounter, I will mine these three commitments for what they suggest about how religious educators might lead change oriented toward hope during these disruptive times. The Monarch butterfly—that glorious species of epic migrators currently experiencing monumental decline—will join my conversation as muse and metaphor.

A Day in a Life: Seeking Redemptive Community

But first, come with me on a brief excursion—an "auto-ethnographic" definition of the vocation of educating for redemptive community.[1] Of course, others would have a different list, but the work of redemptive community is concrete work immersed in the very details of everyday living.

During a 10-day period in between the Jewish holiday, Rosh Hashanah, and ending with Yom Kippur in 2014, I educated *for* and was educated *toward* redemptive community in the following ways:

- In a conservative Southern town, I wrote a letter commending the courage of a racially diverse high school cast who performed *Rent*— the musical celebrating the LGBTQ artist-community's dignity during the HIV-AIDs crisis of the 1990s.

- I copied the youth minister of one of those cast members. That youth minister had been a student of mine 10 years ago when a panel of LGBTQ college students told their stories of coming out and trans-gendering—as seminary students from Ghana, South Korea, and Richmond, Virginia became visibly uncomfortable with the subject matter—but stayed for the complicated conversation that followed.

- I copied that cast member's mom—who happened to confide, while traveling with me on a short-term mission trip to the Dominican Republic last summer, that her youth minister had been particularly helpful to her when her gay son came out of the closet.

- I checked in on a *Facebook* conversation I had begun about whether churches in North America should even be doing short-term mission trips abroad, because even the most carefully prepared can perpetuate "white-savior complex" and inflict long-term harm.

- I attended Friday prayers at the local Islamic Center with two young women—one of them a Suni from Senegal and the other a Shi-ite from Afghanistan—and arranged for another student to get to the synagogue.

- I had a poster made for National Anti-Bullying Day from a piece of art created by a recent graduate who is a practitioner of the afro-Brazilian

1. Auto-Ethnography is a form of research that uses the life of the researcher as the research instrument. It acknowledges the situatedness of knowing and makes transparent the bias existing in all research. Cf. Reed-Danahay, *Auto/ethnography*, and Baker, *Greenhouses*.

religion Candomble. The poster reads "Don't let anyone tell you that you are less than sacred."

- I hosted a bagel bash where students made a prayer wall for a college student whose suspected murderer was not investigated two years ago, even when he had been accused of a sexual assault at the Christian university in our town.

- I completed a 32-hour domestic violence prevention course with my teen-aged daughter, where I learned Christian universities are renowned for under-reporting sexual abuse cases.

- I arranged for 19 interfaith chaplain interns to receive a one-hour training session on suicide prevention, so they will know what to do if a vulnerable student experiences a safe-enough place to share thoughts of self-harm.

- I created a calendar of small groups led by those interns—ranging from Wiccan meditation, to a conservative Christian Bible Study, to a Creating Beloved Community action group, to conversation around the Buddha and the Christ, and to one called Girlfriend Theology.[2]

- I read reflections from a group of seminary interns about the theologically robust experience of creating a Eucharist ritual at a gathering called The Wild Goose Fest, where there are apparently more different kinds of Christians as there are craft breweries in North Carolina.

- I enjoyed a meal cooked over an open fire by an historian who specialized in the eating habits of enslaved people in 1820s Virginia.

- I followed the meal by leading a small group of students and faculty on a walk to the burial site of 61 slaves who worked the 3,200-acre plantation that is now our college.

- I followed that walk by leading 200 robed seniors—with bagpipe accompaniment—to the grave of the daughter of those slave owners, in whose memory this all-women's college was founded.

- I highlighted in yellow a quote from a doctoral student of color that read: this gathering has shown me that "I am not alone in my wild ideas for re-framing theology, but I have found other wild thinkers and doers to curate my wildness, my holy wildness."

2. Cf. Baker, *Girlfriend Theology*, 2002, for a fuller description of this idea.

- I listened to a friend talk about the book he is writing about being both a pastor and a police chief, while bringing his three black sons to adulthood in a small Southern town in the era of Treyvon Martin, Michael Brown, and others.

- I sat on my porch looking at job postings with Evan, an unemployed 21-year-old friend whose journey to college became derailed because of lack of funding and lack of parental know-how.

- I fed my backyard flock of three now fully-grown chickens named— Faith, Hope, and Love—while patiently waiting for the first egg to emerge.

Whew! I am but one religious educator who finds this kind of work to be life-giving. I love the surprises that emerge in the life of pastoral leadership—particularly when that leadership expresses itself across multiple micro-communities of prayer and action.

I know of thousands of others like me, working within their own micro-communities, setting in motion or spurring along acts of justice, mercy, or courage that create pathways for good in the world. It is hard work; it is good work—connecting faith and living. Imagine this list multiplied and morphed. Feel the accompanying assurance that—despite the alarming reports of increasing racism, ethno-centrism, corporate greed, armed conflict, and personal isolation that dominate our media—forces of good are still at work in the world.

Listening to the Voices of the Young

Two contexts of ministry provide the concrete lived reality that help me understand how religious educators might fruitfully equip young people to shape a hopeful future. My foremost context for ministry brought me face-to-face with over 450 young Moseses and Miriams over an eighteen-month period in 2013-14—with young people whose vocations of living faith are emerging. As researcher at the Forum for Theological Exploration, I have been privileged to be learning on three frontlines: [3]

- the changing landscape of congregational life in North America;

3. The Forum for Theological Exploration (FTE) is formerly known as The Fund for Theological Exploration. Celebrating its sixtieth year in 2014, FTE is a leadership incubator for the church and religious academy.

- a complex matrix of young adult hopes, beliefs, and desires for the future; and

- the theological institutions that seek to adapt and respond to tumultuous change necessary if they are to continue equipping leaders for the church and the world.

My other context has been as director of spiritual life at Sweet Briar, a small liberal arts women's college in Virginia.[4] This college has two claims to fame: 3,200 acres of rolling hills along the Blue Ridge mountains regularly rank us as the most beautiful campus in America and the esteemed Dr. Lincoln Brewer. Dr. Brewer is a renowned activist/scholars on the migratory patterns of the Monarch butterfly.

In this *pastoral* pastoral setting, steeped with stories of a species that has experienced dramatic decline in the past five years, I accompany a steady stream of young women coming of age in America. Dr. Brewer attends to monarchs—because he loves them—but also to help chart future correctives for adapting farming practices in Iowa, meeting energy needs in Mexico, and helping backyard gardeners across America create feeding stations along the 3,000 mile migration path. As we pay attention to species in our midst, to the challenges and opportunities they exhibit, we often catch glimpses to how our work can cooperate with and join with the forces of hope and new life.

I, in turn, attend to young Moseses and Miriams for similar reasons—because I love them—and also to help discern future correctives for the multiple micro-communities of prayer and action that support, nurture, and give birth to a similarly fragile sub-species—that young leader of faith. Young leaders—like monarch butterflies—are susceptible to subtle changes that overtime accumulate to change their behavior within a multiple cause/multiple effect ecosystem.

Some of these young people I see daily, as they navigate college crises, but most of them spend a few intense days with us at an FTE retreat and then encounter us again through grants, fellowships and mentoring experiences. These young leaders are nominated by their pastors, their volunteer service-year coordinators, or their seminaries to attend an event

---

4. Shortly after writing this article, I resigned from Sweet Briar to spend more time working with FTE. A few weeks later the college abruptly announced its closing, due to dire financial circumstances.

constructed—we hope—to help them self-organize into ongoing learning communities (kind of like migratory flocks).[5]

Some are pre-seminary, some are in seminary, and some are new pastors—trying to craft a career that allows them to answer their deep call. A smaller percentage of these people are doctoral students of color—people who are called to be the next seminary professors and theological educators, many of whom face enormous obstacles as they navigate the academy constructed of white-male norms while staying true to the redemptive communities that educated and called them.

I call these young leaders Miriams and Moseses because they see and feel and hear the pain of "their people" down in the valley. These are Millennials with hopes and dreams and a profound sense of confidence that they can, indeed, improve the world for "their people"—and they define that community broadly.

A few themes arise as I observe their migratory patterns. I believe we must take seriously both what they encounter and feel as well as for what they long. These are clues to redemptive living.

First, the young Christian leaders I encounter are living the following realities:

- They are suffering from a *culture of anxiety* bred by economic collapse, ecological endgames, and a tangible fear of the zombie apocalypse.

- They are struggling within a *culture of glorified busy-ness* that separates them from the resources of soul care and life-skills for building intimacy and community.

- They are just plain tired of a *churchly set of institutional ways* that hold captive, and sometimes distort, the life-affirming message that has recruited their gaze toward a burning bush.

In turn, these young Christian leaders I encounter cry out for the following:

- *Places to be vulnerable.* Young leaders repeatedly ask for safe-enough spaces to participate in truth-telling and sharing of stories—stories

---

5. Volunteers Exploring Vocation (VEV) is a network of more than eighteen faith-based service organizations where young adults explore the relationship between faith and work during a year of service. http://fteleaders.org/networks/faith-based-volunteer-organizations

of failure and disappointment that help them sit with the pain until a new narrative emerges.

- *Practices of prayer, meditation, sabbath and self-care* to sustain them as they try to change the world. (They are not very picky about where these practices come from. They care a lot, however, that the practices lead into an encounter with mystery.)

- *Holding communities of elder and peer mentors* who will serve not just as priestly presences as their vocations unfold, but also as prophetic thinking partners and advocates as they learn the hard stuff—like how to navigate power, combat inertia, and dismantle bureaucracy.

What does it mean to live in anxiety, busy-ness, and institutional boundaries and, at the same time long for prophetic places and partners where one can be vulnerable, encounter rich practices of faith, and guides on our journeys?

Among this group, over and over, I hear a rejection of words that, as Marcus Borg states, are part of "speaking Christian."[6] Young people find these once rich words have been corrupted and no longer carry the power for change and hope. For example, one young woman literally cried out: "When you say Christ you probably mean something different than when I say Christ. And Christian. When you say that word that doesn't mean me, because you have things attached to that word that don't describe me." Do we need to redefine these words in a public arena? Or do we need new words because the old words have been restricted and ruined?

Or, as another young Christian shared, in response to a blog I wrote about expanding networks of intentional Christian communities on college campuses: "Sounds great, but I could never be part of anything called 'Christian.' I could be part of an intentional interfaith community. But something called Christian?—that would brand me as something I'm not. And put me with people I wouldn't want to be with."

So there are paradoxes we learn from our Moseses and Miriams:

- Millennial Christians feel deeply empowered *and* deeply afraid;

- They love Jesus; but they distance themselves from the words associated with his followers;

- They believe they can change the world, maybe even through the church, but when they arrive on the shores of adulthood, they run into

6. Borg, *Speaking Christian*, 5.

profound disappointment, because changing the world is long, lonely work and institutions entrench. They entrench deeply.

A Framework for Imaging the Future

In light of these paradoxes, we need a framework for imagining the future that provides hope and replenishes the vocational delta—our own and those of the people we teach and lead—when nothing but dry riverbed portends. I find hints in two conversation partners, Otto Scharmer and Meg Wheatley, and two concepts, "emergence" and "principled pluralism." These conversation partners and concepts form a possible way forward for religious educators who want to nurture young people with gifts to lead in uncertain times.

First, to the conversation partners. C. Otto Scharmer, senior lecturer at MIT and co-founder of the Presenting Institute, has been looking at the ways mindfulness can transform business, society and self to create a better global future. He calls for leaders across sectors to tap into a deeper level of humanity. Indeed, he says, "accessing our deepest sources of inner wisdom and the traditions that feed them might be the most important leadership capacity today."[7]

He believes that we cannot transform behavior or systems unless we transform the quality of attention that people apply to their actions within those systems, both individually and collectively. Scharmer writes that "pioneering the principles and personal practices that help us perform a shift in awareness from a focus on individual ego systems to a focus on eco-systems—may be one of the most important undertakings of our times."[8] Practices of mindfulness and attention that connect us to the deepest longings and hopes of humanity are powerful fuel for action.

Margaret Wheatley writes about organizational development, leadership, and change theory—and has been influential in a growing community of learners known as "the Art of Hosting." Her concept of "trans-local learning" describes what "happens when separate, local efforts connect with each other, then grow and transform as people exchange ideas that together give rise to new systems with greater impact and influence."[9]

---

7. Scharmer, *Theory u*, 464.

8. Ibid., 72.

9. Wheatley, *So Far From Home*, 28.

Wheatley argues *against* creating practices/solutions for the purpose of replication; and *for* sharing of ideas in networks of support where ever-evolving practices and solutions get generated for particular contexts—all in a spirit of innovation and design more fitting of a natural system than a mechanized world. She writes: "Many of us harbor the hope that if we do a good job and have evidence of our results, our work will spread and create change beyond our initial project or place . . . such hope places you in the category of saving the world."[10]

But what if we look around and—despite all of our good intentions and all of what liberation theologian Nancy Bedford calls "little moves against destructiveness"[11]—we don't see change occurring? Instead we see increased violence, larger gaps between rich and poor, and exacerbating effects of climate change. How, then, are we to feel, think, and go on acting?

Wheatley proposes a subtle shift away from saving the world, while at the same time moving more deeply into the contextual pockets in which we find ourselves. For her, trans-local learning means increasing attentiveness to the *micro* while simultaneously bringing new attentiveness to the *macro*—the systems in which we operate and the disposition we bring to them.

In fact, the culturally embedded practices Wheatley relates in her book, *Walk Out, Walk On*, resemble the practices of play, imagination, and creativity that we've been mapping and evaluating within the Religious Education Association and its journal, *Religious Education*. Wheatley's work has helped us at FTE ask the question: What if the church is like an old growth forest, like a complex living system with multiple causes and multiple effects, all taking place simultaneously? This theory holds that the greater access a living system has to itself and its resources, the greater its capacity to heal, to adapt, to adjust. [12]

Now to the two concepts: emergence and principled pluralism. Can a living systems theory of change point to effective ways for us to lead and teach in a transitional era like our own, to lead and teach for redemptive community?

In his work with multinational leaders from across sectors, Scharmer illuminates the concept of "emergence" which he's developed in communities

---

10. Ibid., 9.

11. Bedford, "Little Moves Against Destructiveness," 151–181.

12. With the help of Canadian facilitator Chris Corrigan, we at FTE have begun to lead people through an exercise of imagining the different forms of leadership needed in the midst of stages of this living and cycle. www.chriscorrigan.com.

experiencing the complex problems resulting from globalization. Scharmer asks "how do humans respond to the current waves of disruptive change from a *deep place* that connects us to the emerging future, rather than by reacting against the terms of the past, which usually means perpetuating them."[13]

Scharmer and Wheatley are both informed by religious principles—for them Buddhist. Indeed their concepts echo each other in calling out for exactly the stuff religious educators across faith traditions hold. Emergence means we draw on those deepest of resources at the heart of our humanity.

Paired with emergence is the Aspen Institute's idea of "principled pluralism," I see a way forward—toward educating for redemptive community as the twenty-first century progresses. "Principled pluralism" is a term coined by a 25-member panel called the Inclusive America Project that included religious and thought leaders from across all faith traditions in the U.S. "Principled pluralism" articulates the importance of diverse religious traditions self-defining and disagreeing on matters of theology, while also affirming a deep commitment to pursue the common good together in higher education, youth services, media and government. Without blurring or mitigating religious differences, principled pluralism echoes the scholarship of Harvard's Robert Putnam that religious diversity can actually be a source of social cohesion.[14] Partnerships emerge and partnership offers local ways of healing which can tap into the broader work of hope.

Living systems theory, emergence and principled pluralism bring into focus that collectively much of our work as religious educators is about equipping and empowering so many Moses and so many Miriams of all ages—imperfect humans with loads of regret, anxiety, and mental illness. Nonetheless, these Moses and Miriams connect their life's passion with a deep spiritual source and become agents of change (as engineers, teachers, doctors, lawyers, parents, soccer coaches and Christian ministers) along the way.

- What if those young people we know who are sampling from various religious traditions are not doing it merely because they've been enculturated to be consumers at a smorgasbord, but also because they've learned to be wilderness survivors, looking for a little sustenance to get them through another day?

13. Scharmer, *Leading from the Emerging Future*, 3. (italics mine)

14. Alec Hill, "Principled Pluralism" in *The Huffington Post*, www.huffingtonpost.com/alec-hill/principled-pluralism_b_5870132.html (accessed 6/2/2015).

- What if a person's deep investment in a *particular* religious tradition alongside either a playful exploration or a deeply studious investigation of another tradition is *exactly what's* needed if humanity is to find the resources it needs to solve the incredibly complex problems our planet faces?

I believe the innovative approaches necessary for healing the world are indeed only possible if *diverse* populations of *different* kinds of people fed by *varieties* of deep sources and ancient traditions share what they learn from *within* their own micro-communities. I believe religious educators can help birth that process in ways that eschew hierarchy, top-down planning and paternalistic practices in favor of reciprocity, mutuality, and a preferential option for surprise.

Clues for Educating for Redemptive Community

What does that mean for you as you educate for redemptive community in your context? Consider these future-oriented riffs on the three Seymour-ism's I named earlier:

First, as theologians and meaning-makers, religious educators are about the work of helping others become the theologians and meaning makers of their own life experiences. Given this, religious educators and leaders must continue providing resources so people can discover their own voice, individually and communally, and how it reflects God, God's movement, and God's nature. This is analogous to watching the migratory patterns of monarchs and setting up well-placed feeding stations—ranging from tiny backyard gardens to huge fields of native milkweed.

The range is indeed extreme. I'm talking about starting as simple as a group that *today* learns to knit while practicing a watered-down version of the *Ignatian Examin* and *someday* is ready to walk through a study that will form them more deeply in the ways of Jesus. Simultaneously, we must resource young people like Jessie, an undergrad pastoral intern who translated the story of the woman at the well from the original Greek in preparation for a Bible study for the youth group she volunteers to lead.

Some of our young Miriams and Moses need easy on-ramps—low-risk "micro practices" for hungry people who don't know exactly what they're hungry for. Just as important are more sustained practices to feed the rarer subspecies—those people who need accompaniment on deeper dives into ancient traditions where they're already finding the food for which their souls long.

At the same time—wherever we still can—we must continue creating evocative and beautiful spaces *inside and outside brick and mortar* buildings to keep educating children and parents in the practices that build and sustain communities of care, compassion, and justice. This happens when Vacation Bible Schools move into the community garden, or when free dental clinics move into the church basement.

Along the way, I hope we will do what our mentors did: *teach people how to teach people, every small group becoming a leadership lab*, equipping spiritual/activist leaders with practices (such as Praying in Color, Theatre of the Oppressed, or Freedom Songs).

Imagine cadres of young adults who carry this invisible tool kit of pastoral and formative practices to whip out of their back pockets—to lead their peers into meaning-making—after, for example, the bomb goes off at the Boston Marathon or in the aftermath of Michael Brown's death.

Second, our meaning making takes place at the very innermost core of our individual beings, and simultaneously and necessarily at the outer edges of our traditions, where it must do the risky work of ongoing public interpretation if it is to be redemptive. Given this, we continue to steward the multiple creative, imaginative, playful, and beautiful practices that we've learned from the people we've been privileged to have as mentors within our finite field and in the larger, infinite fields into which we migrate for cross-pollination.

And we steward those resources in a way that allows them to change us from the inside out—at the core of our beings, deeply connected to the rivers of life that sustain us—and at the outside borders, the *domus* AND the *polis*— those public arenas where we must do the hard work of listening, translating, compromising, collaborating, waiting, learning and listening again.

Imagine again one of those young adults equipped with the invisible spiritual tool kit. It equips her to reflect on the pain of tragic moments long enough to tap into deep inner wisdom that bubbles up from her unique understanding of an ancient tradition—or multiple traditions. There she begins to improvise with others, who innovate and prototype their way into new solutions and new practices that we may never have imagined, but that may provide alternatives to—for example—a militarized police states and gated communities.

Third, our meaning making takes place not for the sake of inner peace, nor for the sake of preserving our traditions, churches, or institutions—although these are surely sacred purposes—but always for the sake of an aching world and an ever-expanding notions of "who is my neighbor." We attend to Monarch butterflies to learn about our world and our environment. We listen to the voices of the young to see how ways are made to live and even thrive in a world that is anxious, fearful, commodified, and divided. We take clues for deep spiritual resources and watch what is emerging—from God's holiest of spirits.

Conclusion: Holding onto Hope

Given this, we continue to hold hope. I hope that such efforts and methods, while perfectly suited for a particular context, might enter into a wide, wide sea, where they encounter other contexts—alternative creativities. These mash-ups and re-mixes may result not in *better* solutions, but *better-suited solutions* for they are home-grown, created by and for end-users. People are freed to draw on another's work as ingredients in yet another's wild, holy, creative, imagination.

Does educating for redemptive community flow from the source of your life and the center of your calling? Imagine for a moment the many vocational rivers you have watched bubble up—from trickling stream to flowing surge—among the students, parishioners, and neighbors whose vocations you have witnessed awakening.

Imagine your list—your version of 10 days in the life of educating for redemptive community. Now imagine it—not just multiplied—but morphed and mutated by those who've migrated, carrying with them what they learned from you: how to teach others who teach others to make their own meanings and create their own innovative versions of ancient practices. We religious educators are curators of hope. We are curators of knowledge, wisdom, and practices that have no beginning and no end. As we look into the future, I imagine wild, holy migrations. Moseses and Miriams leading us in new ways and in new realities.

Bibliography

Baker, Dori Grinenko. *Doing Girlfriend Theology: God-talk with Young Women.* Cleveland: Pilgrim, 2002.

————. *Greenhouses of Hope: Congregations Growing Young Leaders Who Will Change the World*. Lanham, MD: Rowman & Littlefield, 2010.

Bedford, Nancy. "Little moves against destructiveness: Theology and the practice of discernment." In *Practicing Theology*. Dorothy Bass and Miroslav Volf, eds. Grand Rapids: Eerdmans, 2002.

Borg, Marcus. *Speaking Christian: Why Christian Words have Lost Their Meaning and Power—and How They can be Restored*. San Francisco: Harper Collins, 2012.

Corrigan, Chris. Exercises in seeing the church as a living system. www.chriscorrigan. com (accessed 6/2/2015).

The Forum for Theological Exploration. www.fteleaders.org (accessed 6/2/2015).

Hill, Alec. "Principled Pluralism: The challenge of religious diversity in 21st century America." in *The Huffington Post* (Sept. 23, 2014). http://www.huffingtonpost.com/alec-hill/principled-pluralism_b_5870132.html (accessed 6/2/2015).

Reed-Danahay, Deborah. *Auto/ethnography: Rewriting the Self and the Social*. New York: Bloomsberry Academic, 1997.

Scharmer, C. Otto. *Theory u: Leading from the Future as it Emerges*. San Francisco: Berrett-Koehler, 2009.

Scharmer, C. Otto and Katrin Kaufer. *Leading from the Emerging Future: From Ego-system to Eco-system Economics*. San Francisco: Berrett-Koehler, 2013.

Wheatley, Margaret. *So Far from Home: Lost and Found in Our Brave New World*. San Francisco: Berrett-Koehler, 2012.

————. *Walk Out, Walk On: A Learning Journey into Communities Daring to Live the Future Now*. San Francisco: Berrett-Koehler, 2011.

3

Beyond Band-Aids and Bootstraps

Transformative Mentoring as Redemptive Community

—— *Leah Gunning Francis* ——

RESEARCH IN CHRISTIAN EDUCATION provides an opportunity to examine the interplay between self and other, individuals and communities, and our relationship to God and creation.

Our individual presence in the world must be understood in relation to others. The quest for redemptive community calls us to explore these ideas through the lens of following in the way of Jesus toward the actualization of the kin-dom of God at hand—to walk in the way that leads to wholeness and well-being of all.[1]

My attempt to consider a process for building redemptive community was through my research with African American women. During this project, I paired women from a relatively affluent congregation with women from a homeless shelter in a mentoring relationship. The purpose of these mentoring relationships was to learn more about how community building across social class lines might occur. Through this process, I humbly entered the tepid waters of a social class conversation within the African American community. I do not assert that class conversations are more important than racial justice, or that they should replace conversations about race in the public square. My aim is to engage predominately black congregations in a conversation about race *and* class for the purpose of building redemptive community.

---

1. Seymour, *Teaching The Way Of Jesus*, xvii.

The Intersection of Life and Art

Two primary events that forged my interest in this topic: my upbringing in a middle-class suburban community and the play *In The Blood*, by Suzan-Lori Parks. I am a middle-class black woman. I was born into a middle-class family and raised in a mixed race suburban community in New Jersey. I am a third generation college graduate. My parents and grandparents were married. Our family went to church, traveled, and frequently enjoyed times with our extended family and friends. My siblings and I had more "play cousins" than related cousins for many years because my dad is an only child and my mom is the oldest.

There were at least six public swimming pools in our town of 33,000 people. I had black friends and white friends, black teachers and white teachers, and black neighbors and white neighbors. I could move freely around our neighborhood without a looming threat of violence. Gun violence, or even talking about guns, was virtually non-existent. Of course, there were occasional dust ups among kids, but no one was shot or even threatened to shoot anyone. If a researcher had entered any one of my classrooms, K-12, asking how many people had family members who had been shot, the response would have been quizzical looks.

In addition to being raised in a "village" that supported the well-being of children, I am particularly grateful for parents that were both loving and socially conscious. They poured every ounce of love, nurture and encouragement they had into my siblings and me so that we might develop both deep roots and a wide wingspan. They not only loved us, but they talked to us and listened to us. My dad, a West Philadelphia native, read a couple newspapers daily and insisted on sharing his findings at any random moment, laughing as he recalled the funny stories, and challenging us to think critically about current events.

My mother, a child of the Jim Crow South, held high the racial justice banner in our house. Well-manicured lawns and integrated classrooms did not deceive her nor lull her into a false state of complacency. She, and many of my "other mothers and fathers," were active in the local NAACP and other racial justice efforts. She wasn't afraid to call our mayor or council people to voice her opinion about current or proposed initiatives. When she became fed up with our school board's antics that privileged political favors over the well-being of students, she ran for a seat herself and won. Both of our parents embodied a way of being that let us know that our thoughts and feelings mattered, which helped internalize the notion that *we* mattered—a gift for which I am eternally grateful.

It is through this lens that I sat in a theater one evening and watched a production of *In the Blood* that left me speechless. The play, written by African American Pulitzer Prize winning playwright Susan-Lori Parks, is loosely based on *The Scarlet Letter* where Hester Prynne is now Hester LaNegrita, an illiterate African American homeless woman.[2] She and her five children lived under a bridge in an unnamed city in the United States. Throughout the play, Hester maintained that if she could just "get her leg up" she could adequately care for herself and her children. Realizing she could not transcend her social and economic transition alone, Hester tried to "get her leg up" by soliciting help from a physician, social worker, and a pastor, each of whom crossed professional boundaries and took advantage of her.

The ideological claims made by the social worker and pastor struck me. The social worker, named "Welfare," was a middle-class African American woman who smugly described herself as having "Money in my pocket, clothes on my back, teeth in my mouth, womanly parts where they should be, hair on my head, husband in my bed."[3] She made clear sociocultural distinctions between herself and Hester. However, when challenged by Hester that Welfare didn't understand her plight, Welfare suddenly adamantly disagreed that she couldn't understand by saying "I'm a woman too! And a black woman *just like you*. Don't be silly."[4]

A few scenes later the pastor, named "Reverend D," an African-American man who doubled as pastor and street preacher, stood on a street corner imploring his listeners, "Let the man on the soapbox tell you how to pick yourself up . . . how all your dreams can come true. You can pull yourself up." He prided himself as someone who had "pulled himself out of that never ending gutter."[5]

Welfare's over-identification with Hester's plight and Reverend D's claim that he "pulled himself up" out of adversity represents two fallacies that can be detrimental to the social, psychological, economic and spiritual well-being of individuals and communities. Even though Welfare is a black woman, she is not "just like" Hester. Welfare implied that their shared race was their social equalizer. However, the socioeconomic disparities between

2. Parks, "In The Blood."

3. Ibid.

4. Ibid.

5. Ibid.

them created a chasm of difference that rendered many of their life experiences separate and unequal.

Reverend D may have overcome adversity. However, it is unlikely that he "succeeded" solely as a result of his own efforts but was assisted by someone along the way. The notion of a "self-made" man or woman is incongruent with an understanding of human relations and success that render us interdependent of each other. As a result, an uncritical examination gives a false impression that any notion of achievement is an autonomous enterprise.

Welfare and Reverend D espoused an embedded belief that an individual, regardless of socioeconomic circumstances, can autonomously improve his or her condition. The social and theological implications of these notions are profound. How might a predominately African American congregation seek to build understanding and community across class lines? What are the educational methods that should be employed? How might these efforts expand a congregation's identity and imagination to consider transformative social change, rather than temporary solutions?

Beyond Band-Aids and Bootstraps

Congregations seek to address the issue of homelessness in myriad ways. Some utilize their space to provide temporary shelter. Others prepare and serve meals. Still others assemble food baskets at Thanksgiving, collect toys during Christmas for homeless families, and make clothing and monetary donations to homeless shelters. The primary approach of those congregations who attempt to address the issue of homeless is what I call a "band-aid" approach. A band-aid approach provides a temporary solution (i.e. temporary shelter or food) but does not address the social, political, and economic forces that contribute to the situation of homelessness. Nor does a band-aid approach allow the recipient to participate in his or her own empowerment. A band-aid approach to homelessness is *important and necessary* for meeting the immediate need of food/clothing/shelter, but is insufficient for longer-term personal or social transformation.

The other ideology—the "bootstraps" one—suggests that personal achievement is as simple as pulling oneself up by the bootstraps. It negates the role of communal support people receive on the road to success, and presupposes that everyone has the exact same tools and resources to achieve their goals. It is one of the most dangerous ideologies present in our society, allowing those in positions of power to promulgate an ethos of blaming others for not achieving while conveniently overlooking the financial, cultural, social, and emotional support they may have had along the way. I have heard several people describe it as "pretending you hit a homerun when you started the game on third base."

Few, if any, African American women start the game of life on third base. My effort was an attempt to name this reality while utilizing the resources and strengths of African American congregations—namely its women. While some think of this kind of work as "giving back" to others, I framed as "giving forward." "Giving back" can reinforce the "I'm better than you" mentality. "Giving forward" directs ones gaze in a particular way. I wanted to bring the plight of homeless black mothers *in front of* the women in the congregation as we reflected on appropriate theological and practical responses. It is insufficient to merely shame people by saying "You need to give back. Remember where you came from?" because many middle-class black women were never homeless or unable to meet basic needs.

I prefer to challenge black middle-class women to critically reflect on their support systems that enabled them to be where they are today. In *Unfinished Business*, ethicist Keri Day offers an important critique of the relationship of black congregations to poor black women. She rightly criticizes faith-based initiatives as inadequate because they do not address the structural inequalities faced by poor black women.[6] These initiatives are more congruent with a band-aid approach, rather than systemic action.

I often wondered about the extent to which some middle-class black women embraced the idea of systemic injustice. If a woman does not believe it exists, she will more likely resort to blaming poor people for their circumstances. What type of educational process might enable her to see systemic injustice differently? How might this become part of the educational process in congregations?

Transformative Mentoring Community

My approach was to form a transformative mentoring community that surpasses the band-aid approach and embraces an ethic of are and community. In turn, it rejects the bootstraps mentality, naming it antithetical to the cultivation of redemptive community. The underlying assumption is that no individual achieves any measure of success without the assistance of

---

6. Day, *Unfinished Business*, 47.

others. My research focus was on the effects of the transformative mentoring community for educating congregations for social transformation.

The transformative mentoring community I designed was comprised of black middle-class mothers from a relatively affluent congregation and black mothers who were living in a homeless shelter with their children. The ten-week community building process included anti-bias training with the women from the church, private meetings between the women from the church and women in the shelter, and large group conversations with women from both places.

Although I name this process as mentoring, I learned that they were more *cojourners* than mentors and mentees. Pastoral theologian Marsha Foster Boyd writes "Cojourners are spiritual companions brought together on a common path for a particular time."[7] These relationships were not formed so the women from the church could swoop in and "save" the others. Rather, they were encouraged to engage in conversations that the women from the shelter might find helpful. The women from the church were encouraged to do more listening than talking, that they might learn and understand more about the person they encountered.

A transformative mentoring community is primarily constructed by using a womanist approach to Christian education. Womanist theology brought to the forefront the oppression of black women in general and the social and theological dissociation between black and white women in particular. Extensive work has been done on the role of race and gender; however, there has been minimal investigation into the implications of class among black women and its meaning for educating Christians for social transformation.

Seymour and Miller describe a task of Christian education as "facing into the world:"

> Facing into the world is the task of Christian education. Through Christian education we face into the world, explore the deepest meaning of our lives, engage one another, and partner with a God seeking wholeness and meaning for all of life. Facing into the world includes social analysis as people look at the forces that shape their lives and seek to understand the context within which they live and breathe. We must take seriously the issues and problems that are both at the edge of consciousness and those that are staring us in the face. Hope to engage a world that seems to be falling apart

---

7. Boyd, "WomanistCare," 200.

cannot be accomplished if we deny the brokenness of the world or if we run away in despair. Hope arises as we face into the world.[8]

As we "face into the world," we open ourselves to the possibility of finding meaning and purpose for our lives while seeking to transform that which is broken to wholeness. Religious educator Mary Elizabeth Moore asserts that religious education can be transformative when it begins at the intersections of our lives—the place where the past (traditions and values), present (individual and communal realities), and the future (dreams, expectations, concerns) converge.[9]

A transformative mentoring community is shaped by a process of Christian education that begins at the intersection and embodies a collective turning toward the hope of seeking a communal solution. I examine the concepts of home, hope, and hospitality as foundational to a transformative mentoring community.

Home

The word home has deep theological roots in the Christian tradition. From scriptures to songs, home is often used to demonstrate an eschatological hope of a place of eternal residence.

There are also familiar phrases such as "home is where the heart is" or Dorothy's immortal declaration "there's no place like home" in *The Wizard of Oz*. These statements suggest a dual nature of the word home. "Home is where the heart is" points to the notion that home is a state of being, a place where one's authentic self can thrive and flourish. To be at home is to know your essence, accept yourself, and love yourself unconditionally. To be at home with oneself is to live with purpose and intentionality. To be at home with oneself is to live as one created in the image of God and in partnership with God.[10]

How might congregations make space for people to feel "at home" and have the freedom to fully be themselves? Educator Carol Lakey Hess proposes the concept of conversational education as a means to honor women's connectional experiences while celebrating the differences among them.

8. Seymour and Miller, "Agenda for the Future," 121–122.

9. Moore, *Educating for Continuity and Change*, 109–111.

10. While I underscore the importance of a physical home to one's sense of security, stability and comfort, I utilize the word home as a state of being and not only a place of dwelling.

The church's educational ministry can create an environment where people can engage in "hard dialogue" and "deep connections" in an attempt to foster authentic relationships.[11]

This form of communication occurs between ourselves, others, and God. It is vital for true relationality. Hess' notion of "hard dialogue" gives room for honest expression while remaining connected with others. Hard dialogue between ourselves and others does not give us permission to disrespect, silence, or dismiss others. Instead, hard dialogue invites us to consider the multiplicity of viewpoints while having the freedom and confidence to voice our own. Hard dialogue with our tradition allows for critical engagement of biblical and theological texts. Finally, hard dialogue with God emboldens us to ask the hard questions and not blindly submit to our circumstances, fostering a deeper connection with God and a clearer understanding of ourselves in relations to God and others.[12]

Nelle Morton in *The Journey is Home* recounts her experience of journeying from home and the lessons she learned early in the feminist movement. For Morton, home was not a physical place, rather "Home is a movement, a quality of relationship, a state where people seek to be 'their own,' and increasingly responsible for the world."[13] Homemaking as an act of meaning making of one's life and existence, offering acceptance as well as an awareness that we are in the process of becoming. Homemaking is a continuous process rather than a specific destination. One's understanding of self can evolve and deepen through new experiences and opportunities.

An aim of the transformative mentoring community was for the members to do what was needed to feel "at home" in their relationships. Becoming "at home" is predicated upon the way in which community members utilize agency and express voice, care for self and the community, and construct meaning from their relationship.

Hope

In her book *Trouble Don't Last Always*, Womanist educator Evelyn Parker introduces "emancipatory hope" as a vehicle for engaging African American youth in the work of dismantling oppressive systems of injustice.[14]

---

11. Hess, *Caretakers of Our Common House*, 41.

12. Ibid., 183.

13. Morton, *The Journey is Home*, xix.

14. Parker, *Trouble Don't Last Always*, 17.

Personal and social freedom from all forms of domination is the aim of emancipatory hope.

In *Hope in the Holler*, Womanist theologian Elaine Brown Crawford listened to the stories of selected African American women, from slavery through emancipation to the civil rights movement, to explicate their understanding of hope as it arose out of a context of suffering, abuse, and pain. She suggests that hope enabled them to move beyond endurance and survival toward the transformation of unjust social structures.[15] She argues that Womanist theology must be attentive to the particularities of hope of black women—"humanity, voice, freedom and equality." Crawford urges the critical exploration of black women's firsthand accounts to define what hope means for them today.

Womanist theologian Delores Williams understands the Kingdom of God as a "metaphor of hope" for those who seek to right relationships with others and God and place love above everything else. To see Jesus as the one who offers a new vision for humanity, grounded in an ethic of love, gives hope that the world as we know it is not the way it has to be. Williams' perspective reinforces the interconnected, communal aspect of humanity, and emphasizes the context of black women's experience as valid and important for theological construction.

Williams, Parker and Crawford offer insightful perspectives to a womanist discussion of hope. For Williams, God can be seen in a new way that empowers healing and transformation. Parker offers how "emancipatory hope" seeks the dismantling of unjust social structures and encourages human flourishing. Crawford challenges us to consider how hope has functioned in the lives of black women.

Hope is a critical aspect of a transformative mentoring community because of its aim to empower the entire community to "see in a new way." All members of the community can be empowered to participate in transformation—community members can become sources of hope for each other.

Hospitality

Hospitality calls us to welcome the stranger or "the other"—to act in ways that care for someone else's well-being in addition to our own. Hospitality involves risk: we extend ourselves to others perhaps unsure of how they

15. Crawford, *Hope in the Holler*, xii.

will respond. Will they be suspicious of our motives? Are we clear about our motives? Do we extend hospitality only to receive something in return? Henri Nouwen addresses the nature and scope of hospitality that is instructive for building redemptive community. He writes:

> Hospitality, therefore, means primarily the creation of free space where the stranger can enter and become a friend instead of an enemy. Hospitality is not to change people, but to offer them space where change can take place.... The paradox of hospitality is that it wants to create emptiness, not a fearful emptiness, but a friendly emptiness where strangers can enter and discover themselves as created free; free to sing their own songs, speak their own languages, dance their own dances; free also to leave and follow their own vocations. Hospitality is not a subtle invitation to adopt the life style of the host, but the gift of a chance for the guest to find his own. [16]

Nouwen's description attends to the transformative aspects of hospitality for both guest and host. There is no need for domination and control, rather a place where difference can be encountered, explored, and embraced. Furthermore, Elizabeth Conde-Frazier argues for relinquishing a "central vision" in order to embrace multiple perspectives that move us toward God's shalom—communities of justice, equality and compassion. [17]

Hospitality is a Christian practice. Christine Pohl posits that hospitality is a lens through which we interpret the gospel. [18] Two biblical texts are important for her: the parable of the Good Samaritan (Luke 10:25–37) and the judgment upon the nations (Matt 25:31–46).

Both stories illustrate Jesus' commitment to be in solidarity with those who are marginalized or ostracized. Jesus' definition of a neighbor is not determined by where one lives in proximity to another. A neighbor is one who shows compassion and gives care to one in need. Pohl embraces the "subversive and countercultural" nature of Christian hospitality, "Because the practice of hospitality is so significant in establishing and reinforcing social relationships and moral bonds, we notice its more subversive character only when socially undervalued persons are welcomed." [19]

---

16. Nouwen, *Reaching Out*, 71–72.

17. Conde-Frazier, "From Hospitality to Shalom," 206.

18. Pohl, *Making Room*, 8.

19. Ibid., 62.

Although the term "hospitality" may invoke images of hosting the family Christmas dinner or opening one's home for the PTA officer's meeting, hospitality as an expression of the gospel provides service for the benefit of others and not for the purpose of political, social or economic gain. Hospitality provides a context where cultural and class boundaries can be transcended and persons can be recognized by their human worth.

There are certain levels of risk in offering hospitality to others. Rejection is possible.

Hospitality requires the initiator to become vulnerable when opening him or herself to another. We expose dimensions of our character, values, or emotions that we often closely guard out of fear of exploitation, ridicule, or exclusion. Another risk associated with offering hospitality is the possibility that the host may change, or be transformed.

However, the stories of strangers have the power to enable us to "see in a new way," challenge our assumptions and practices. N. Lynne Westfield's study with an African American women's literary group revealed the role of resiliency in the face of racial, gender and class discrimination and offered a "new way of seeing" these gatherings as more than just a fellowship time, but a way of nurturing and cultivating resiliency among its members.[20] Strangers became friends through the sharing of stories as understanding and respect emerged. A new way of seeing for the stranger may be their hope for a better quality of life. A new way of seeing for the host can lead to a more genuine and relevant practice of hospitality.

Transformative Education and the Mentoring Communities

Transformation occurs at the intersection of home, hope, and hospitality by enabling mentors to "see anew" aspects of themselves, others and societal structures. I posit that a transformative mentoring community is an approach to Christian education as transformation that affirms when we confront our prejudices/stereotypes and create space (hospitality) for people to be who they are (home), we make room for the possibility to see anew (transformation) and engage in empowering action (hope).

---

20. Westfield, *Dear Sisters*, 41.

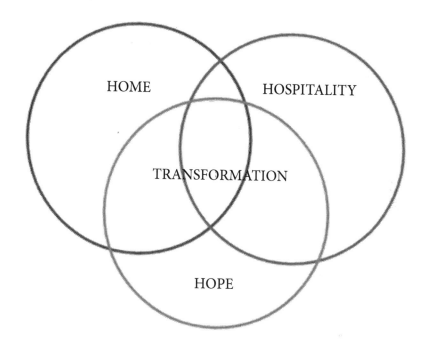

Confronting prejudices and stereotypes

During the mentoring training session, the mentors were paired off to discuss images or words that emerge upon hearing the phrase "homeless black women." The descriptions they reported were "poor, lots of kids, wandering, unsettled, single mom, lack of family support, bad choices, uneducated, lazy, unemployed, underemployed, lack of skills, shady and sad." Each of these responses revealed unexamined assumptions about homeless black women. The mentors articulated that these images are often fed through the media. They were challenged to reflect on their own beliefs and attitudes about homeless black women.

For the mentors, these descriptions represented what Belenky, et.al describe as received

Knowing—information that mentors had uncritically received from other sources of authority, like the media.[21] It was clearly "received" since none of the mentors had ever been homeless or personally knew a homeless woman. They constructed their opinions based on other people's beliefs

21. Belenky, et. al, *Women's Ways of Knowing*, 35.

and attitudes. Such relying on exterior, uncritically examined sources of information makes it more difficult to develop one's own sense of authority and judgment. A second challenge of these unexamined assumptions is that they can negatively impact the relationship between the mentors and mentees. Mentors could draw negative conclusions about the mentoring process before it even begins.

In this instance, the mentors articulated perspectives that were not based on their own experiences or other reliable sources. While I did not assume these views were deeply held beliefs, they readily emerged. The very fact that the women were willing to participate in the study suggested that they were open to new insights and challenging stereotypes. Indeed, confronting prejudices and stereotypes is a critical component of a building community since prejudices and stereotypes thwart the development of relationships. Moreover, the presence of prejudices and stereotypes also revealed the importance of acknowledging the class divide.

Acknowledging the class divide

The mentors' descriptions of "homeless black woman" reveal an important class divide. The thrust of Womanist theology is to attend to the ways racism, sexism, and classism impact the lived experiences of black women. In this instance, classism is experienced quite differently for the mentors and mentees. While the impact of classism in the black community needs further exploration in both Womanist theology and Christian religious education, Womanist theologians Marcia Riggs and Emilie Townes offer constructive directions.

For example, offering a critical reconsideration of debate that focuses on determining whether race or class is more determinative of black flourishing, Riggs argues that race and class must be held in tension because both have contributed to the "complex situation of black oppression."[22] Given the widening socioeconomic gap between affluent and lower income blacks, Riggs asserts, "The assimilative acceptance of this competitive class consciousness on the part of Blacks has led, in effect, to the ethical dilemma of the internal dimension of black oppression: competitive individualism versus intragroup social responsibility."[23] The result has been a "false black

22. Riggs, *Awake, Arise & Act*, 14.
23. Ibid., 19.

consciousness and sympathy without empathy."[24] False black consciousness renders the black self as solely autonomous and not self-in-relation to others. "Sympathy without empathy" emphasizes middle and upper class blacks' resistance to working with lower class blacks for communal liberation. Riggs contends that all blacks are embedded in an unequal social system and should discern the meaning of communal responsibility by addressing the causes of social stratification and working toward intra-race reconciliation.

Riggs' argument is of particular importance to my notion of a transformative mentoring community. First, Riggs, and I, affirm the importance of race and class in understanding the experience of black people in the United States. I do not believe that conversations about race should be replaced with conversations about class. What I seek to articulate is the need to address the implications of class within the black community as it relates to the black church and social transformation.

Second, Riggs' attentiveness to the way in which some middle class blacks have adopted the values of individualism and competitiveness to the detriment of communal thriving is instructive for thinking about the aim of a transformative mentoring community. A transformative mentoring community seeks to embody the principle that all of humanity is interrelated. For my project, transformative mentoring community is focused on the experiences of black women together.

Third, a transformative mentoring community seeks to transcend a false black consciousness or "sympathy without empathy" to acknowledge the reality of the mutually liberative benefit of communal engagement. I argue that the practice of a transformative mentoring community has the potential to transform all who participate. Sympathy is replaced with Hess' notion of empathetic caring. Empathetic caring makes room for honoring others' differences without losing one's sense of self. As a result, connectedness can exist within the boundaries of difference.

In turn, Emilie Townes' work is helpful for understanding how the promulgation of individualism has impeded black communal thriving. Townes rightly asks "In advocating a bootstrap approach to economic upward mobility, does the mainstream African American church also condone a socioeconomic order that places some of its actual or potential constituency in a moral no-win situation?"[25]

24. Ibid., 87.
25. Townes, *In a Blaze of Glory*, 133.

Townes challenges the black church. Any theological reflection that characterizes the current economic system as just cannot connect with those who reside in poverty in the context of the wealthiest nation in the world. Likewise, a theological reflection that acknowledges injustice but only focuses on reform also does not connect with those most inflicted. Townes calls for the black church to proclaim a spirituality that attends to the interrelatedness of God to humans, and humans to humans for the purpose of relationship building. God's spirit beckons us into relationship with God and one another to bear witness to God's activity in the world—which includes the quest for justice. For her, the black church must respond to the disparities faced by African Americans in the criminal justice system, access to healthcare and economic structures. For Townes, social critique and engagement for the purpose of communal thriving is essential for the black church's witness in the world.

Townes' approach is helpful for understanding a transformative mentoring community because it denounces the bootstraps approach that undermines authentic expressions of community and underscores the role of God's spirit in this reconciling work. This type of reconciling work calls us into relationship with one another in such a way that we can create space (hospitality) for people to be who they are (home), and thereby open the possibility to see anew (transformation) and engage in empowering action (hope).

Learning from Mentoring Communities

In the transformative mentoring community that the women and I developed together, one of the common experiences of the mentors was that they could all identify something they learned about themselves, and the critical self-reflection enabled them to adjust their mentoring to try to better meet the needs of the mentee. Some might assume that the goal for this type of mentoring would be the transformation of the mentee.

I did not attempt to try to "measure" transformation for the mentor and mentees. However, the research revealed signposts that pointed toward transformation. All involved were able to "see anew." The transformative space in the center of the interlocking circles of home, hope and hospitality is fluid, not fixed. As the interlocking circles change, so does the potential for transformation. Since home, hope, and hospitality are practices, they can be reformed and reshaped. As a previous formation dissolves it makes way for new relationships to occur that may not have happened had not the previous relationship existed. In this sense, these transforming relationships have the capacity to build upon one another while honoring each one as a distinct whole.

Making Space: The Practice of Hospitality

In a transformative mentoring community, the practice of hospitality should create a space that allows for change to occur. We need intentional dialogue in our congregations about the nature, purpose and expectations of community. A first invitation to dialogue is extended to the congregation by virtue of God's call to justice, mercy, humility (Mic 6:8), and love (Luke 10:27). Congregations are called to be places that embody an ethos of God's justice, mercy humility, and love. Hospitality is essential. Congregations need to be places where all are welcomed and belong.

The mentors and mentees created space for each other in ways that were risky, yet filled with potential. They were invited to share of their time, wisdom and energy with each other in a way that sought to empower each of them. They were also invited to be open to the ways in which they, too, might be transformed.

What I learned about the practice of hospitality is that it is a call of faith and a call to faith. It is an invitation to "go without knowing." Yes, they were aware of the logistical arrangements and facts. However, the unknown lay in the more intangible aspects of the mentoring relationships such as rapport, process, and outcome.

The mentor and mentee invitation as a call of faith is grounded in the understanding of embodying God's love and justice as expressions of our faith. The mentor invitation as a call to faith was asking them to commit to and believe in a process that had no definitive outcome and no certain response. The call to faith was a call to believe that their participation may have a positive impact on another person's life.

Free to Be: The Practice of Home (making)

Once the space has been created for the "other" to enter, the potential now exists for home making, where persons can be their authentic selves. Gwen, a mentor, and Gail, a mentee, illustrate this point. When Gwen "saw" Gail, she, in turn, caught a better glimpse of herself. Gwen said, "I wanted to concentrate on the person, not on [the] surrounding[s]." As a result, Gwen was able to focus on listening to Gail and following her lead. Gail affirmed this reality by saying her mentor was "someone who cares about me and listens to me." Gwen also learned she did not have to do; she could just be. She was enough, her presence and personhood—not just what she could do.

Sharon Daloz Parks' notion of home is helpful to describe Gwen's experience of being "at home" with herself. She writes, "To be at home is to be able to make meaning of one's own life and of one's surroundings in a manner that holds, regardless of what may happen at the level of immediate events."[26] Gwen and Gail are an example of the bi-directionality of transformation. Although Gwen's emphasis was on helping Gail feel "at home," she, in turn, found meaning and purpose through this experience for her understanding of herself, which likely enabled her to be a more effective mentor.

Gwen's experience illustrates an important learning for the practice of home (making): being is as important as doing. In other words, who you are matters. How you interact with others makes a difference. This learning is important for congregations and individuals who desire to engage in a relational type outreach but fear not knowing what to "do." I have learned that a community that cares can be well suited for the practice of home (making). To understand this caring, I return to Carol Lakey Hess' three aspects of caring: empathetic, conversational, and prophetic.

Empathetic caring requires a willingness to listen to a person's story without making judgments about his or her actions, choices and opinions. Empathetic caring acknowledges that one shoe size does not fit all, and that we cannot judge others based on our own experiences. To be empathetic is not to falsely identify with experiences that are not one's own, but to have the integrity to accept the differences in another's journey without negating one's own. In turn, empathetic caring can evoke reflective responses about one's own life journey after listening to the story of another.

Two mentors, Brenda and Angela, reflected on how their interaction with their mentees challenged them to reflect on their own privileges and advantages. Brenda said she now had "sensitivity to a lifestyle I wouldn't have thought about before, and caused me to see things from a different perspective." Brenda's openness to Betty's story created conditions where Betty could feel accepted and honored as a person, and not a label. Angela displayed empathy by questioning her own ability to respond to adversity. She asked "If I'd have had as many barriers in my life and if I had been

---

26. Parks, *Big Questions, Worthy Dreams*, 34.

knocked down like that, would I be as positive as I am and motivated?" Her empathy unlocked the door for conversational caring.

Conversational caring ensures that all voices are honored and heard. If one's voice is not honored, they will be afraid to speak or feel anger. Voice, or the expression of one's authentic self, plays an important role in establishing genuine caring relationships. While I cannot assess the extent to which conversational caring happened in the mentoring relationships, the potential for conversational caring is greater when empathy is present and participants feel safe to share.

Once empathy has been established and a conversation started, prophetic caring can become part of the equation. Prophetic caring calls us to care enough to hold each other accountable. While this may seem counterintuitive while creating a space where people can feel "at home," it is necessary if genuine relationship is to be established. Conflict may be a starting point for genuine relationship to emerge because all participants feel free to name their feelings or challenges and seek viable solutions to their problems. Conflict can also be the point where people take flight. However, if the participants are willing to stay the course and endure the thorny places that accompany change, then the potential for them to become more of their authentic selves exists.

Empowering Action: The Practice of Hope

The practice of hope in a transformative mentoring community is both a call and a response. The "call" is to hope in God (Ps 42:5) and God's ability to "make a way out of no way." This call is grounded in a belief that even in the midst of a seemingly hopeless situation, there is reason to hope because of God's presence among us (Ps 46:1–7). Hope in God is particularly important to the work of a transformative mentoring community when we see the overwhelming number of homeless black women with children. How does one maintain hope in spite of the staggering statistics? Hope in God can empower people to seek solutions rather than ignoring the situation.

For a congregation, mentors, and mentees who participate in a transformative mentoring community, both notions of success and failure have to be reconsidered. One might assume that a "successful" mentoring relationship is one that enables a homeless woman to find permanent housing and work. However, that is a difficult challenge that often requires many layers to be unraveled. While the hope is for the mentees to ultimately find housing that they are able to financially maintain, the reality is that it may not happen during the time of the mentoring relationship.

Instead, I advocate a "new way of seeing" success. The fact that all of the mentors and mentees were willing to spend intimate time with strangers is an indicator of success. None of the women were financially compensated for their participation yet they still, by and large, committed to the mentoring relationships. What this reveals is they participated because they wanted to, and they believed that their participation might make a difference. This is an important practice of hope.

The belief that one's involvement can make a difference cannot be underestimated. This belief gives strength to all persons involved, even when results are limited. Some may call this planting a seed, while others describe it as watering a flower, however I call it empowered co-journeying. An empowered cojourner is one who walks beside another as she seeks to become all that God intended. The task is not for the empowered cojourner to "fix" her companion, rather to constructively accompany her on the journey. This relationship is not intended to last indefinitely, rather for a season. The hope is that there will be changes, but the participants cannot predetermine that outcome. It is only found in the journey. Hope is continuing to cojourner and believe that God is able to do more than we can see or imagine.

Implications for a Womanist Christian Religious Education

Intentional-engagement is a viable process of Christian education. The mentors identified their participation as being informed by their understanding of what it means to be a Christian, and it reinforced their belief that the church needs to do more on behalf of those who are on the margins of society. A congregation who embraces the identity of a transformative mentoring community has the potential to "see anew" their role in the struggle for justice.

Olivia Stokes and Grant Shockley advocated intentional-engagement models of Christian education that sought to affirm the value, worth and dignity of African Americans in the midst of the struggle for racial equality.[27] Their models explicitly related black people's identity as both Christian and African American. Unfortunately the struggle for racial equality

27. See Foster and Smith, *Black Religious Experience*, 75–123.

continues today, even with the election of President Barack Obama, the first black man to hold the office of the president of the United States.

However, I would like to add another dimension to the quest for justice. A transformative mentoring community approach seeks to affirm the dignity and worth of all black people, but it also recognizes that there are intra-race class distinctions that need not be overlooked. If middle class and affluent black congregations are going to take seriously the empowerment of poor black people, they must examine the ways in which unexamined social class disparities impede their quest for social transformation.

The black middle and affluent class must examine class privilege and the ways we benefit from it. Racial equality remains a vital struggle for all African Americans (i.e. legal, economic, education). The task of Christian education is to combine attention to racial equality and economic realities. Unexamined class privilege must not undermine any efforts toward hospitality and social transformation. Class investigation has been limited in womanist theological discourse and needs to be expanded. If the black church is to have a prophetic voice committed to the liberation of all black people, then it first has to acknowledge that middle/affluent blacks are not fighting all the same battles as poor blacks. Some, but not all. While most middle class blacks are economically vulnerable (just like most other middle class people in the US), they have access to a network of social capital that is unavailable to most poor blacks.

Black churches, which are predominately middle class, need to acknowledge their class realities as they consider their role in social transformation. Black churches have to move beyond the band-aids or bootstraps mentalities. Womanist Christian education is primed to help them do so. It must challenge these realities in black churches. The emphasis on individualism is to our peril. None of us has achieved any measure of success without the assistance of others.

Ultimately, I assert that black congregations have to move beyond the band-aid approach and the bootstraps mentality in order to embrace a mode of engagement that is reflexive, relational and empowering if we are to build redemptive community. Christian religious education is a vehicle through which we can begin this process.

Bibliography

Belenky, Mary Field, et. al. *Women's Ways of Knowing: The Development of Self, Voice and Mind*. New York: Basic, 1997.

Boyd, Marsha Foster. "WomanistCare" in *Embracing the Spirit: Womanist Perspectives on Hope, Salvation and Transformation*, Emilie M. Townes, ed. Maryknoll, NY: Orbis, 1997.

Conde-Frazier, Elizabeth. "From Hospitality to Shalom" in *A Many Colored Kingdom: Multicultural Dynamics for Spiritual Formation*, Elizabeth Conde-Frazier, S. Steve Kang and Gary A. Parrett, eds. Grand Rapids, MI: Baker Academic, 2004.

Crawford, A. Elaine Brown. *Hope in the Holler*. Louisville: Westminister John Knox, 2002

Day, Keri. *Unfinished Business: Black Women, the Black Church, and the Struggle to Thrive in America*. Maryknoll, NY: Orbis, 2012.

Foster, Charles R. and Fred Smith. *Black Religious Experience: Conversations on Double Consciousness and the Work of Grant Shockley*. Nashville: Abingdon, 2003.

Hess, Carol Lakey. *Caretakers of Our Common House*. Nashville: Abingdon, 1997.

Moore, Mary Elizabeth. *Educating for Continuity and Change*. Nashville: Abingdon, 1983.

Morton, Nelle. *The Journey is Home*. Boston: Beacon, 1985.

Nouwen, Henri J.M. *Reaching Out: The Three Movements of the Spiritual Life*. New York: Image, 1975.

Parker, Evelyn L. *Trouble Don't Last Always: Emancipatory Hope Among African American Adolescents*. Cleveland: Pilgrim, 2003.

Parks, Sharon Daloz. *Big Questions, Worthy Dreams: Mentoring Young Adults in Their Search for Meaning, Purpose, and Faith*. San Francisco: Jossey-Bass, 2000.

Parks, Suzan-Lori. "In The Blood" in *Red Letter Plays*. New York: Theatre Communications Group, Inc., 2001.

Pohl, Christine D. *Making Room: Recovering Hospitality as a Christian Tradition*. Grand Rapids, MI: Eerdmans, 1999.

Riggs, Marcia Y. *Awake, Arise & Act: A Womanist Call for Black Liberation*. Cleveland: Pilgrim, 1994.

Seymour, Jack L. *Teaching the Way of Jesus: Educating Christians for Faithful Living*. Nashville: Abingdon, 2014.

Seymour, Jack L. and Donald E. Miller, "Agenda for the Future" in *Mapping Christian Education*, Jack L. Seymour, ed. Nashville: Abingdon, 1997.

Townes, Emilie M. *In a Blaze of Glory: Womanist Spirituality as Social Witness*. Nashville: Abingdon, 1995.

Westfield, N. Lynne. *Dear Sisters: A Womanist Practice of Hospitality*. Cleveland: Pilgrim, 2001.

4

From Sabbath Schools to Freedom Schools

Christian Vocation and the Power of Voice

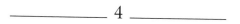

Reginald Blount

IT WAS IN SEMINARY that I was introduced to African American sociologist W.E.B. Dubois and his classic work *The Souls of Black Folk*. In his critically acclaimed 1903 work, Dubois writes:

> The Negro is a sort of seventh son, born with a veil, and gifted with second-sight in this American world, a world which yields him no true self-consciousness, but only lets him see himself through the revelation of the other world. It is a peculiar sensation, this double-consciousness, this sense of always looking at one's self through the eyes of others, of measuring one's soul by the tape of a world that looks on in amused contempt and pity. One ever feels his twoness, an American, a Negro; two souls, two thoughts, two unreconciled strivings, two warring ideals in one dark body, whose dogged strength alone keeps it from being torn asunder. The history of the America Negro is the history of this strife, this longing to attain self-conscious manhood, to merge his double self into a better and truer self.[1]

This notion of double-consciousness really resonated with me because it gave me language concerning my community, the African American community. I realized that my concern was for a community that found itself measuring who it was more by the judgment of the dominant society rather than by God, their Creator. DuBois' words gave language to my ministry. His words helped me to see my ministry as one that would aid

1. Dubois, *The Souls of Black Folk*, 3.

the Black church in understanding who it was individually and collectively in the eyes of God. I saw my ministry as one called to "equip the saints for ministry" (Eph 4:12), helping them to claim and embrace an understanding that God calls all of humanity into existence for a meaningful and necessary purpose, that no one enters this existence by chance; that God calls all persons into being to serve in partnership and covenant with God toward the continued renewal of God's creation. Because of DuBois' influence, I have for most of my academic career strived to make the case that *the purpose of Christian Education is to set people free—free to be children of God and free to be co-creators with God.*

In this article I want to unpack this statement by first sharing the theological anthropology that undergirds it through the themes of vocation and voice. I will go on to demonstrate how it has been engaged historically and presently through the Sabbath schools of the Reconstruction Era, the Freedom Schools conducted during the Summer of 1964, and the Freedom Schools as they are run today through the work of the Children's Defense Fund. Finally, I will close with why this approach to Christian education is important.

Vocation and Voice

My belief that the purpose of Christian education is to set people free—free to be children of God and free to be co-creators with God—is rooted in Brazilian educator Paulo Freire's understanding of "ontological vocation."[2] Freire, in his work, *Pedagogy of the Oppressed*, advocates for a way of teaching and learning that attempts to transform oppressed persons by awakening in them an innate calling or vocation to become more fully human. Freire suggests that this innate calling is ontological. Oppressed persons, in their quest for liberation, are to see themselves " . . . engaged in the ontological and historical vocation of becoming more fully human."[3]

I define ontological vocation as the intimate and inseparable bond between existence and calling. It is predicated on the belief that God calls all of humanity into existence for a meaningful and unique purpose. It further argues that one's identity most fundamentally resides in the knowledge and

2. This notion is explored in greater detail in my unpublished Candler School of Theology Master's thesis: "Ontological Vocation: A Constructive Theological Quest," 1995.

3. Freire, *Pedagogy of the Oppressed*, 26.

belief that one is called by God to serve as God's agent, steward, and partner in the caring and re-creating of God's creation.[4]

Walter Brueggemann helps me further explain my understanding of ontological vocation as he shares the following:

> The notion of identity questions is based on the assumption that the person in and of himself/herself, has within his/her body an identity to be embraced. Identity questions are by definition, self-focused ...identity for a person is given in the call of the other One. It is the voice of the initiating One who calls human persons to a destiny. Maturation is coming to terms in free ways with that which galvanizes God's purpose in our lives.[5]

Brueggemann, in an attempt to explain how in our humanness we can participate in covenant with God and with others, suggests that in light of covenantal relations, all identity questions transform into vocational questions: "The dynamic of humanness is in the interaction between the One who *calls* and the one who is *called*. The agenda between them is also a *calling*."[6] Vocation is not, for Brueggemann, a job or a profession but a reason for being in the world that is also related to God's purposes: ". . . we are not speaking here of our mother's ambition for us or an institutional blueprint for our lives, but of the dreams of the One in whom we are grounded . . . . Vocation means we are called by this One who is calling us to service . . . ."[7] Ontological vocation can best be understood, then, in terms of "who I understand God has called me to be."

Howard Thurman serves as another critical voice in illuminating this notion of ontological vocation. Thurman's thoughts on religious experience, commitment (which he defines as the interrelationship between freedom and responsibility), and self-worth clearly articulate what I try to convey concerning ontological vocation. Thurman's understanding of commitment rises out of his understanding of the nature of freedom, responsibility, and life. Liberation, synonymous to freedom for Thurman, is a key theme of his theology. Thurman's sense of liberation focuses inward on those elements that keep persons from believing they are free. Thurman asserts that

---

4. I must credit James Fowler for being an instrumental voice in shaping my understanding of vocation. Cf. Fowler, *Becoming Adult, Becoming Christian* and *Faith Development and Pastoral Care.*

5. Brueggemann. "Covenanting as Human Vocation," 125.

6. Ibid., 125.

7. Ibid., 126.

one is not free if outside forces dictate. He writes, "The basis of one's inner togetherness, one's sense of inner authority, must never be at the mercy of factors in our environment, however significant they may be. Nothing from outside can destroy a man until he opens the door and lets it in."[8]

For Thurman, inner freedom cannot be conquered unless there is also internal acquiescence. A person achieves liberation or freedom " . . . when the human person as being is no longer defined, limited, and controlled by external powers, but is creatively empowered by those principles of self-determination that allow one to actualize total realization of being irrespective of the limitations imposed upon him by external milieu."[9] A person can be denied liberty, which Thurman defines as an external force that is bestowed or withheld according to the will, judgment, and behavior of someone other than self, whereas, freedom is internal and cannot be denied unless it is forfeited, for freedom is an individual's birthright from God.[10]

This discipline of commitment involves, for Thurman, the "inescapable demand of surrender," not to other individuals, but to God. Thus, for Thurman, commitment means:

> . . . that it is possible for a man to yield the nerve center of his consent to a purpose or cause, a movement or an ideal, which may be more important to him than whether he lives or dies. The commitment is a free, self-conscious act of will by which he affirms his identification with what he is committed to. The character of his consent is determined by that to which the center or core of his consent is given.[11]

Thurman argues that a discipline of commitment provides answers to the classical existential questions "Who Am I?" and "What Do I Want?" The answer to "Who Am I?" begins with a person recognizing his/her fragmentary nature. Many of us, Thurman suggests, are like the man Jesus encountered who, when asked his name, cried out "My name is Legion." Thurman postulates what Legion could have further stated: "This is the pit of my agony. There are so many of me, and they riot in my street. If only I could know who I Am—which one of me—then I would be made whole

8. Thurman, *Deep is the Hunger*, 80.
9. Stewart, *Being, God, and Liberation*, 87.
10. Fluker, *They Looked for a City*, 36.
11. Thurman, *Disciplines of the Spirit*, 17.

again. I would have a center, a self, a rallying point deep within me for all the chaos, until at last the chaos would become order."[12]

For Thurman, one finds self, one becomes a whole person, one answers the question "Who Am I?," when one chooses to surrender all the collective fragments of oneself that one knows of to God, resulting in one being connected with a commitment big enough to demand one's all. One's encounter with God provides an opportunity to center and focus one's fragments on those things that God wills for one.

The question "What Do I Want?," Thurman suggests, flows directly from how one answers "Who Am I?" If one has surrendered his/her fragmentary nature to God and has chosen to have that nature focused on God's will and purpose for his/her life, then Thurman suggests that the answers to "What Do I Want?" will be intimately connected to God's will and purpose. Thurman states: "When a man faces this question put to him by life, or when he is caught up in the necessity of answering it, or by deliberate intent seeks an answer, he is at once involved in the dynamics of commitment. At such a moment he knows what, in the living of his life, he must be for and what he must be against."[13]

For me then, Christian education is about helping persons embrace an ontological vocational understanding that their lives have meaning and purpose. It is helping persons embrace an understanding that they are called by God to serve as God's agent, steward, and partner in caring for and re-creating God's creation. It's echoing the writer of Jeremiah who writes, "Now the word of the Lord came to me saying, 'before I formed you in the womb I knew you, and before you were born I consecrated you . . .' (Jer 1:4–5)." It also echoes the writer of Ephesians who writes, "For we are what he has made us, created in Christ Jesus for good works, which God prepared beforehand to be our way of life (Eph 2:10)."

If the purpose of Christian education is to set people free, this seems to presuppose that there are situations and circumstances that hinder, bind, and obstruct the ability to live free. If we embrace an ontological vocational understanding that we are called to serve as God's agents, stewards, and partners in the caring and re-creating of God's creation, Christian educators then have the call to equip those entrusted to their care with this understanding and to serve as catalysts in assisting to remove situations and circumstances that hinder, bind, or obstruct the ability of people to live

12. Ibid., 27.

13 Ibid., 34.

free. I believe Christian educators can best do this by aiding those learners entrusted to their care to transform their voice.

Russian scholar Mikhail Bakhtin argues that embodied in one's "voice"—talk, speech, conversation—is one's "perspective, conceptual horizon, intention, and worldview."[14] Embodied in one's voice is their way of seeing the world, how they see others and themselves. He says that embodied in one's voice, in one's speech, is their identity or their sense of personhood. He says our voice takes shape out of the dialogue of voices that take place in the communities that influence us. When we speak, "when we produce an utterance, at least two voices can be heard simultaneously."[15] Voices never exist in isolation of other voices.[16]

We make meaning when the voice of the listener responds to the voice of the speaker. Our worldview and our sense of who we are begin taking shape as we engage an inner dialogue that is in response to the outer dialogue we have. When we engage in subsequent conversations, the statements of our previous conversation partners are omitted, but they are still present invisibly; their words are not there, but traces left by the their words have a determining influence on all our present and visible words.[17]

When we attempt to aid a person grappling with the question of identity and their purpose for being, it is important to know what voices have served as their conversation partner(s). The voices with which a person interacts may have a profound effect on their self-image or identity.

If Christian educators took seriously the voices shaping the lives of their learners and were committed to the purpose of "setting people free," I believe they would do it in a way that Old Testament scholar Walter Brueggemann described as he reflected on 2 Kings 18–19:

> The king of Assyria sent troops to Jerusalem and threatened King Hezekiah. Rabshakeh, whom the king of Assyria sent, confronted the Israelites at the wall of the city and mocked them for putting trust in their king and their God. Hezekiah's representatives implored the Assyrians to speak to them in Aramaic, not in the language of Judah "in the hearing of the people (2 Kgs 18:26)." But the Assyrians refused, for it was in their best interest to have all the people hear and understand their challenge: "Do not let Hezekiah

14. Wertsch, *Voices of the Mind: A Sociocultural Approach to Mediated Action*, 51.

15. Ibid., 13.

16. Ibid., 51–52.

17. Ibid., 88.

make you rely on the Lord by saying, 'The Lord will surely deliver us, and this city will not be given into the hand of the king of Assyria' (2 Kgs 18:31)." But the people did not answer, for their king had commanded that they put their faith in God. King Hezekiah was distraught and "tore his clothes, covering himself with sackcloth, and went into the house of the Lord (2 Kgs 19:1)." Then he sent his intermediaries and the senior priests to consult with the prophet Isaiah, who counseled them not to surrender and assured them that the Lord would indeed protect Jerusalem from the siege. It happened as the prophet had claimed, and the city was spared.[18]

This passage, among other interpretations, reflects the power of voices and the places where conversations take place. In this passage, conversation takes place at the wall and behind the wall. At the wall, public or societal conversation takes place. It is primarily the conversations of the dominant culture, and Brueggemann suggests, when this discourse is operative, the discourse of the marginalized has no privilege or advantage.[19] Behind the wall, transforming and empowering discourse is taking place. The community behind the wall has the power to shape the conversation versus having it imposed upon them by those on the wall.

Brueggemann would say this is not a call for the church to become separatist, but it is a call for the church to provide safe space for transformation and renewal to take place, using the language and culture of the "behind-the-wall" community and not that of the dominant culture. The church must become once again a "behind-the-wall" community, a community that offers alternative dialogue for those yearning for a healthy and liberating sense of self.

I want to demonstrate what this looks like through the role of Sabbath Schools during the time immediately following the end of the enslavement of persons of African descent, the Freedom Schools of 1964, and the Children's Defense Fund Freedom Schools today.

---

18. Vogel, *Teaching and Learning*, 7. Cf. Brueggemann, "The Legitimacy of a Sectarian Hermeneutic: 2 Kings 18–19," 3–34.

19. Brueggemann, "The Legitimacy of a Sectarian Hermeneutic: 2 Kings 18–19," 6.

Sabbath Schools and Freedom Schools as
Agents of Redemptive Community

Historically, one of the roles the Black church played in the lives of the people entrusted to its care is that of educator and nurturer. Through its role as educator and nurturer, the Black church was very influential as the socializing agent of self-worth and self-esteem building. The church reminded persons of African descent that they were somebody, even if the dominant society worked hard to convince them otherwise. In times when African Americans were denied educational opportunity and were the object of blatant disrespect and abuse (both physically and emotionally), the Black church not only provided moral and intellectual instruction, but through such instruction offered and instilled a sense of self-worth and self-determination within adults and youth. The Black church used education as a critical vehicle to help fashion a sense of ontological vocational understanding, a sense of identity and purpose among community members who daily experienced the degradation of their personhood.

Education historian James D. Anderson, in his work, *The Education of Blacks in the South, 1860-1935*, provides an insightful view of the importance of education to the newly emancipated persons during the period of Reconstruction. Anderson's historical accounts portray an emancipated people thirsty for freedom and, for many, education served as the gateway.

Anderson and others argue that the quest to be literate and educated finds its roots in the strivings of enslaved people to be educated during the antebellum era. Thomas H. Jones, a North Carolinian enslaved in the mid-nineteenth century, learned to read in the back of his enslaver's store. Jones is quoted as saying, "It seemed to me if I could learn to read and write, this learning might, nay, I really thought it would point out to me the way to freedom, influence and real secure happiness."[20] Jones endured three brutal whippings in efforts to conceal his pursuit for literacy.

To these enslaved persons, who were willing to take the risk of experiencing beatings or even death, education was viewed as a gateway to freedom and liberation. African Americans carried that passion into Emancipation and the Reconstruction period. Albert Raboteau, in his work, *Canaan Land: A Religious History of African Americans*, states the following:

20. Anderson, *The Education of Blacks in the South, 1860-1935*, 16–17.

Harriet Ware, a white Northern Teacher in Port Royal, Virginia, noticed the religious awe with which the freed people viewed education. Attending a funeral in 1862, she observed: "As we drew near to the grave we heard all the children singing their A, B, C, through and through again, as they stood waiting round the grave . . . . Each child had his school-book or picture book . . . in his hand—another proof that they consider their lessons as in some sort religious exercises." The desire to read the Bible for themselves—the Bible the slaveholders had so long misrepresented to them—motivated a good many former slaves to seek education.[21]

What became a primary goal of many of the ex-enslaved persons was the desire to start their own schools and have responsibility for shaping them. All across the South were "self-sustained" or "native" schools, where ex-enslaved people were training themselves and others how to read and write. One form of these "self-sustained" schools was the Sabbath Schools.

In many communities, Sabbath Schools served as the precursor to free or public schools. These church-sponsored schools functioned primarily in the evenings and on weekends, reaching thousands who could not attend school during the day. These schools equipped their students with basic literacy skills along with Christian instruction.

Anderson points out that Sabbath Schools remained viable well into the post-Reconstruction era. Anderson reports that, in 1868, the African Methodist Episcopal Church had enrolled 40,000 students in its Sabbath Schools; by 1885, the enrollment had dramatically increased to 200,000 students receiving "intellectual and moral" instruction.[22] In fact, all the educational institutions of the African Methodist Episcopal Church at that time functioned under a moral, religious and liberal arts philosophy that was intended to prepare African Americans for life.[23] Self-determination, a vital part of the socializing process, was the primary agenda within the educational movement of the ex-slaves.

Sabbath Schools emerged out of a belief that if the barrier of illiteracy was removed, former enslaved persons could live free. It started with a belief that former enslaved persons were people of worth. Christian education served as a socializing agent to remind persons they were created to live free, and living free demanded they dismantle the obstacle that illiteracy created.

21. Raboteau, *Canaan Land*, 64.

22. Ibid., 13, 15.

23. Williams, *The Christian Recorder*, 50.

This same understanding was at the heart of the creation and conducting Freedom Schools in the summer of 1964. The Mississippi Freedom Schools were developed as part of the 1964 Freedom Summer civil rights project organized by The Council of Federated Organizations, which was an umbrella civil rights organization that included as its members SNCC (Student Nonviolent Coordinating Committee), CORE (Congress of Racial Equality), NAACP (National Association for the Advancement of Colored People), and SCLC (Southern Christian Leadership Council).

Freedom Summer was essentially a statewide voter registration campaign in the state of Mississippi, where the framers called for one thousand volunteers to assist in the undertaking. During the planning of the Freedom Summer project, SNCC Field Secretary Charles Cobb proposed a network of "Freedom Schools" that would foster self-awareness, self-determination and political participation between Mississippi elementary and high school students, in addition to offering literacy development and discussions. His proposal was accepted and in March 1964 a curriculum planning conference was organized in New York under the sponsorship of the National Council of Churches.

The purpose of the curriculum design conference was "to design a progressive 'civic curriculum' to explore new styles and democratic methodology that would enable students 'to see their worth, their dignity, and . . . forge out programs to liberate themselves . . . [to] develop a critical attitude . . . which allows them to think, to question, . . . to begin to re-evaluate themselves,' especially in terms of Mississippi's oppressive social order (SNCC, reel 38)."[24]

George Chilcoat and Jerry Ligon, in their article, "Discussion as a Means for Transformative Change: Social Studies Lessons from the Mississippi Freedom Schools," state that:

> Freedom schools became a font of real activity during the Mississippi Project. Students began to have a sense of themselves as people who could be taken seriously. They were encouraged to talk, and their talk was listened to. They became articulate about what was wrong and what changes should be made. Connections between curriculum and personal experience were made as students studied the realities of conditions in Mississippi and the effects of those realities on their lives. Students discovered that they were real human beings and that they could alter realities by

24. Chilcoat and Ligon, "'We talk here. This is a school for talking,'" 171.

taking action against the injustices that kept them 'unhappy and impotent.'[25]

The Freedom School movement was rebirthed in 1992. According to the historical outline shared on the Children's Defense Fund's website:

> The Freedom Schools movement was reborn in 1992 under the leadership of Marian Wright Edelman (who was part of the volunteers in 1964) and the Children's Defense Fund's Black Community Crusade for Children (BCCC) program to advance this transforming vision of education for all children through the *CDF Freedom Schools* program . . . . In the words of Dr. John Hope Franklin, honorary co-chair of the *BCCC* program, we want our children 'to appreciate fully the artistic, moral and spiritual values that will bring to them much of their heritage of the past and make it possible to pass them on to their successors. [We want to help our children develop] an understanding and appreciation for family, for their own rich heritage derived from their African forebears as well as their American experience, the kind of understanding that will simultaneously provide them with roots and wings.[26]

The following statements also serve as the core beliefs that guide the vision and mission of the Children Defense Fund's Freedom Schools:

- All children are capable of learning and achieving at high standards.
- Culture and community conditions influence child learning.
- Appreciation and knowledge of one's culture engenders self-worth and the ability to live in community with others.
- Education, teachers, and mentors are transformative agents.
- Literacy is essential to personal empowerment and civic responsibility.
- Effective teaching requires planning, creativity, and implementation, with reflection and processing.
- Learning communities that offer a sense of safety, love, caring, and personal power are needed for transformative education.
- Classroom discipline and management are integral parts of instructional practice.

25. Chilcoat and Ligon, "Discussion as a Means for Transformative Change," 218

26. http://www.childrensdefense.org/programs-campaigns/freedom-schools/about/core-beliefs-philosophy.html (Accessed 10/25/2014).

- Parents are crucial partners in children's learning and need supports to become better parents.

- As citizens, children and adults have the power to make a difference in their communities and be advocates for themselves. [27]

Freedom Schools are being conducted in 107 cities, and the majority of the sites are housed and run by local congregations. Many of these congregations see the conducting of Freedom Schools in their community as a vital part of their Christian education ministry. The curriculum and pedagogical methods of Freedom Schools allow these congregations to engage in the "behind-the-wall" formation that Brueggemann describes.

Historically, the Black church was instrumental in meeting many needs within the African American community, primarily through the church's role as Christian educator and nurturer. The Black church served as the socializing agent of self-worth and building self-esteem as well as the compelling voice that declared that every black life mattered—that every black life had purpose. In times when African Americans were denied educational opportunity and were the object of blatant disrespect and abuse (both physically and emotionally), the Black church attempted and often succeeded in serving as a catalyst in helping African Americans reconcile their double-consciousness and embrace an understanding of self-importance and worth. If we believe that the purpose of Christian education is to set people free, then Christian education must continue to commit itself to being that catalyst in removing barriers that keep persons from fulfilling their call to serve as God's agent, steward, and partner in the caring and re-creating of God's creation.

Bibliography

Anderson, James D. *The Education of Blacks in the South, 1860-1935*. Chapel Hill: University of North Carolina Press, 1988.

Blount, Reginald. "Ontological Vocation: A Constructive Theological Quest." Master's Thesis, Candler School of Theology, Emory University, 1995.

Brueggemann, Walter. "Covenanting as Human Vocation." *Interpretation* 33 (1979) 115-129.

———. "The Legitimacy of a Sectarian Hermeneutic: 2 Kings 18–19." In *Education for Citizenship and Discipleship*, edited by Mary C. Boys. New York: Pilgrim, 1989.

27. Ibid.

Chilcoat, George W., and Jerry A. Ligon. "Discussion as a Means for Transformative Change: Social Studies Lessons from the Mississippi Freedom Schools." *Social Studies* 92:5 (September 2001) 218.

Chilcoat, George W., and Jerry A. Ligon. "'We talk here. This is a school for talking.' Participatory democracy from the classroom out." *Curriculum Inquiry* 28:2 (Summer 1998) 171.

"Core Beliefs and Philosophy," www.childrensdefense.org/programs-campaigns/freedom-schools/about/core-beliefs-philosophy.html.

Dubois, W. E. B. *The Souls of Black Folk.* New York: New American Library, 1969, 1903.

Fluker, Walter. *They Looked for a City: A Comparative Analysis of the Ideal Community in the Thought of Howard Thurman and Martin Luther King, Jr.* Lanham, MD: University Press of America, 1989.

Fowler, James. *Becoming Adult, Becoming Christian: Adult Development and Christian Faith.* San Francisco: Harper & Row, 1984.

———. *Faith Development and Pastoral Care.* Philadelphia: Fortress, 1987.

Freire, Paulo. *Pedagogy of the Oppressed.* New York: Continuum, 1982, 1970.

Raboteau, Albert J. *Canaan Land: A Religious History of African Americans.* New York: Oxford University Press, 1999.

Stewart, Carlyle F., III. *God, Being, and Liberation: A Comparative Analysis of the Theologies and Ethics of James Cone and Howard Thurman.* Lanham, MD: University Press of America, 1990.

Thurman, Howard. *Deep is the Hunger.* New York: Harper & Row, 1951.

———, *Disciplines of the Spirit.* Richmond, IN: Friends United Press, 1977.

Vogel, Linda. *Teaching and Learning in Communities of Faith.* San Francisco: Jossey-Bass, 1991.

Wertsch, James V. *Voices of the Mind: A Sociocultural Approach to Mediated Action.* Cambridge, MA: Harvard University Press, 1993.

Williams, Gilbert Anthony. *The Christian Recorder: Newspaper of the African Methodist Episcopal Church.* Jefferson, NC: McFarland & Co., 1996.

$$5$$

Embodied Redemption

Implications for a Transforming Community

—— *Débora B.A. Junker* ——

THE CURRENT INTERNATIONAL LANDSCAPE leaves little doubt that we are living in a tumultuous era steeped in fear, violence, economic instability, and a variety of insecurities. In the midst of such circumstances, faith communities are challenged to ponder what types of interventions they might develop in order to cultivate a genuine yearning to become a living vision of God's peaceable kin-dom,[1] an embodiment of God's redemptive community. The path toward redemption cannot be an abstract endeavor; rather, it should be a path intentionally designed, inviting us to face human contradictions, to confront the prescribed borders that separate us, to contest unfair arrangements, and to expand the possibilities that may lead us in the quest toward transformation. Drawing insights from Paulo Freire's work and inspired by the Judeo-Christian prophetic tradition, this chapter seeks to imagine and articulate some educational principles the faith community needs to embrace in order to become an embodied redemptive community.

Poets and Prophets

Poets and prophets are special people in that they are gifted to see human experience with empathy, discernment, and imagination. Poets are not afraid to venture outside orthodox claims, using metaphorical and evocative images to express what which they see and how such realities are

---

1. A word coined by Ada Maria Isasi-Diaz to avoid the hierarchical and imperialist connotations associated with the word 'kingdom.' See Isasi-Diaz and Tarango, *Hispanic Women*.

registered within them—how they process that which is seen, lived, experienced. Poets have the ability to open new horizons and layers of awareness that may subtly illuminate what has hitherto been perceived faintly because they have the ability to see beyond what is apparent to the eyes. Through their aesthetic contemplation of ordinary life events, they touch the souls of those who read or hear them.

Prophets, on the other hand, are the ones who—having the sensitivity of poets—take measures to denounce oppressive structures and injustices, announcing what needs to be done in order to improve the conditions of life for all. According to Rabbi Abraham Heschel, "what poets know as poetic inspiration, the prophets call divine revelation," and both are "endowed with sensibility, enthusiasm, and tenderness, and, above all, with a way of thinking imaginatively." For Heschel, "prophecy is the product of poetic imagination"[2] and such sensitive imagination is not only desired, but very much needed in order to re-imagine new topographies for our current cultural landscape.

The prophet's task, thus, can be rooted in the effort to promote an alternative consciousness for the people who have been convinced to accept their fate, the suffering and oppression imposed on them, by those who use an ideological discourse intended to justify their status quo. Such a task may help to re-envision realities that at first glance may seem doomed to suffering and brokenness. As Walter Brueggemann says, the prophet's work "is nothing less than an assault on the consciousness of the empire, aimed at nothing less than the dismantling of the empire both in its social practices and its mythic pretensions."[3] Heschel considers that the prophet has a twofold task, "not just as a censurer and accuser, but also a defender and consoler" in bringing the world into divine focus.[4] Thus, the prophet is not simply a person that harshly challenges the power structures and the evil actions that subjugates people. Rather, the prophet is a person vested with agency who is able to sustain dialectically his/her own critical vision and the insights of the poet, and yet, is able to deliver his/her bold message with hope and imagination, two elements that nurture and sustain each other.

Hope can often be interpreted as a driving force both for poets and prophets, the dynamic energy that fuels, inspires, and motivates them to embrace their vocations. Certainly, hope is voiced and announced

2. Heschel, *The Prophets.* Vol.2, 147–148.

3. Brueggemann, *The Prophetic Imagination*, 2nd Edition, 9.

4. Heschel, *The Prophets: An Introduction.* Vol.1, 24.

frequently by poets and prophets—those who possess an insistent sense of the possibilities for transformation, wonder, and perhaps even joy—but hope is also potentially present in each human being as a necessary means of personal survival, as well as a collective effort to advance the elements that may transform our reality. Being so, hope is closely related to the absence of what one longs for, that which is somewhat out of reach. Hope produces a certain conviction that solving this shortage is possible, which in turn prompts a series of actions that forge creative alternatives to build new models for emancipatory realities. Conversely, hope cannot be dependent on the self-centered and self-indulgent. Rather, it should take the shape of a cooperative enterprise motivated by a collective consciousness that forges redemptive hope.

In this chapter, I present some viewpoints intended to elicit substantive conversation around the question of how faith communities can contribute to the formation of people so that they develop critical minds, nurture compassionate hearts, and become agents of peace and justice—the embodiment of the Gospel message—as members of a redemptive community. In doing so, particular attention will be given to the significance of the prophet's role and the undeniable relevance of hope, as important constructs of a redemptive community in the midst of our chaotic times.

From Hope-less to Hope-filled Communities

Even the most hopeful vision or interpretation of our reality cannot dissipate the deep brokenness and despair that affect many communities of our world today. Unquestionably, the past and present terror humanity has witnessed does not allow us to forget the darkness in which we live. We are reminded daily of perverse realities with increasing levels of poverty, high rates of unemployment, concentration of wealth in a few hands, cultural patterns of imposition on a planetary scale (dictated by entertainment industries), new forms of colonialism, the violation of human rights, wars, xenophobia, racism, violence against fellow humans and the planet, and a growing lack of hope in the possibilities of change. In confronting these circumstances, we may feel our strength vanishing and our bodies becoming exhausted as we wait for changes to happen. Out of such overwhelming reality, our utterance becomes even stronger when we hear the cry "I can't breathe"[5] any longer.

5. I use this expression to represent the excessive violence we have seen taking

Considering the challenges of a society marked by complex and ambiguous parameters, it is important to consider hope as an important axis to guide and sustain the renewal of the educational task and the role faith communities need to undertake while facing such complex and perplexing realities. Despite some views that try to depreciate and disqualify hope by attributing an escapist or illusory characteristic to it, hope needs to be understood as an asset to confront the challenges of contemporary contexts. In this regard, hope is not passive or static, but rather a dynamic movement that propels us not to conform to 'the way things are.' As Brazilian educator Paulo Freire points out, hope is "an ontological need," demanding an ongoing process "anchored in practice," connecting human existence and the necessary struggle to make it better. He helps his readers understand that:

> The matrix of hope is the same as that of possibility of education of human beings—becoming conscious of themselves as unfinished beings. It would be a flagrant contradiction if human beings, while unfinished beings and conscious of their unfinished nature, did not insert themselves into a permanent process of hope-filled search. Education is that process. . . . There has never been a greater need to underscore educational practice with a sense of hope than is today.[6]

Understanding hope as a vital element in our individual and social existence, Freire advises us " . . . not to allow hopelessness and despair to conquer us, because they are both the consequence and the cause of inaction or immobilism."[7] As a corrective to apathy and paralysis, Evelyn Parker suggests "emancipatory hope"[8] as means to challenge the hegemonic relations and to embody God's vision of equality for humankind. Further, she adds that this emancipatory hope is intrinsically intertwined with the religious and political dimensions of human existence, and the quest to overcome racial, economic, social, and political domination through a process of critical consciousness. For that reason, we need an education in hope—an emancipatory hope—to enable us to thrive, having the courage

---

place in the USA and beyond. Eric Gardner died because of a choke hold (New York, July 17, 2014). Michael Brown was fatally shot (Ferguson, MO August 9, 2014). The mass kidnapping of 43 students (Mexico, September 26, 2014). The killing of 132 children by Taliban gunmen (Pakistan, December 16, 2014). These are but a few horrific examples among many others that go unrecorded every day.

6. Freire, *Pedagogy of Indignation*, 100.

7. Freire, *Pedagogy of Hope*, 3.

8. Parker, *Trouble Don't Last Always*, 146.

to fight for change until we see the evil dismantled and defeated. This kind of hope inspired the biblical prophets to perform their roles as spiritual leaders.

In the Judeo-Christian tradition, prophets are portrayed as the spokespersons of God. They are paradoxical people whose words can bring judgment or hope, distress or comfort. According to Heschel, the voice of God reverberates in the voices of prophets, and it is their task to convey a divine view from their own perspective and social location. Heschel posits that "the prophet is not only a prophet. He [sic] is also a poet, preacher, patriot, statesman, social critic, moralist."[9] In his analysis of prophetic utterances, Heschel indicates that the vital experience of the prophets is to be in "communion with the divine consciousness which comes about through the prophet's reflection of, or participation in, the divine pathos.[10]" Such harmony enables the "prophet to hear God's voice and to feel God's heart."[11] Prophets are inclined tirelessly to hear God's voice and to feel God's presence and, at the same time, their ears are attuned to the cries of the needy; their eyes are opened to see oppressive forces; and in their hearts pulse the unequivocal desire to transform inhuman realities.

One book that exemplifies the conjunction of both poetic and prophetic expression is the book of Isaiah. Latin American biblical scholar Severino Croatto, states that Isaiah is one of the most influential books in Judeo-Christian tradition, with its sublime poetic and symbolic languages. In are contained memorable liturgical texts able to nurture hope among those who suffer. According to Croatto, from a Christian perspective, the book has "set" the prophetic tone of Jesus' ministry. Furthermore, he recognizes that Isaiah's book has invigorated theological understanding of God's liberating project in the history of the oppressed.[12]

A full background of the book of Isaiah[13] is beyond the scope of this chapter, but it suffices to mention that Isaiah lived during a time of great

---

9. Heschel, *The Prophets: An Introduction.* Vol.1, x.

10. Ibid, 219. Heschel defines 'pathos,' concern for the world, as the very ethos of God. He says, "Pathos is, indeed, righteousness wrapped in mystery, togetherness in holy otherness."

11. Heschel, *The Prophets: An Introduction.* Vol.1., 26.

12. Croatto, "Composición y Querigma del Libro de Isaias," 2000.

13. Most scholars believe that the book of Isaiah is a combined work that includes the sayings of at least three prophets from different eras. The first 39 chapters are credited to the prophet Isaiah, who lived in the eight century B.C.E. See Stanley, *The Hebrew Bible,* 425–479.

adversity that affected life in its geopolitical, economic, cultural, and religious dimensions. During the exercise of his prophetic activity, Isaiah witnessed the new Assyrian empire reaching its maximum power, and Judah submitted to imperialist threats and humiliated by her situation of dependency. Isaiah's narrative is sharply critical of power elites who enjoy lives of luxury while ignoring or abusing the poor and needy in their midst, and rulers who engage in violence and corruption. In this narrative, however, it is also possible to identify the call for people to repent intertwined with messages of hope and encouragement—two important forces in reshaping a threatening reality.

One passage from the book of Isaiah that has rich images of hope and joy in the midst of brokenness is found in chapter 9:2–7. In the scope of this essay, verse 2 brings an interesting perspective: "The people who *walked in darkness have seen* a great light; those who lived in a land of deep darkness—on them *a light has shined* (italics mine)." For Isaiah, the light shines in the land of darkness. Jürgen Moltmann, distinguished German theologian, posits that this passage from Isaiah shows the prophet who "announces what he sees and hopes for in the language of assurance, as if they were already present."[14] The prophet is able to imagine a different reality despite the imposed reality of the dominant culture. From that scenario, still stained with blood and injustice, a cry of hope is proclaimed: where death rules, life will triumph, where there were once tears, now there is joy. The prophet announces a message of encouragement for those facing life's hardships, showing them that, in the midst of that adversity which creates despair and darkness, God walks with God's people, and helps them to overcome their tribulations.

Isaiah's vision speaks to the plight of his people, but it relates to the experiences of people everywhere: the imprisoned, the immigrant, the silenced, the poor, and all victims of violence, abuse, and terror no matter what is used to justify the violence perpetrated against them—the color of their skin, religious affiliation, gender, ideologies, or their political convictions. By virtue of the extensiveness of times and places to which the prophet's vision speaks, we trust that God is present in the midst of our current trials and turbulence. Thus, this passage offers communities of faith some insights to reflect on what it means to embrace hope in times of darkness, and to reflect on the pedagogical implications for faith communities

14. Moltmann, *The Power of the Powerless*, 29.

that seek to embody the vision proclaimed by Jesus—to bring hope and truth to a darkened world.

In places where light is weak, the eyes try to adjust themselves in the darkness until they can see. Those who are sightless know that the light is not just "out there" but "within," and they learn to see in novel ways—by hearing, smelling, feeling, and imagining—in the same way poets who see beyond what is apparent to the eye. During the dark times of our lives, if no effort is made to keep on "seeing" the light, our sight might become weak and atrophied. Hence, it is necessary to keep adjusting the eyes in order to perceive that light is still shining even though in a very elusive way. Surely, in a context fraught with contradictions, inadequacies, and complex problems, to recognize light in the midst of darkness is an action that requires all of our senses to be able to see beyond a present reality, based not only on individual senses, but also with our senses stretched and enriched by the integration of the senses of the group.

Moltmann suggests that to live with hope means to be able to search and choose possibilities. He says, "Realism teaches us the sense of reality. Hope, however, teaches us a sense of possibility. As long as we live, we can transcend our reality and move forward in the realm of possibility."[15] Implicit in his idea is the notion that being able to see light in dark times requires more than eyesight; it implies seeing possibilities where perhaps there are apparently none. It also requires fighting against a 'discourse of impossibility' intended to make possibility unviable. This is what Freire calls a "fatalist discourse" that immobilizes history and fades away our resistance, making us give up the "permanent and almost always uneven struggle for justice and ethics."[16] Instead of feeling immobilized by the offensive violations of human rights and social injustices, we must become "patiently impatient," as Freire suggests:

> The question then lies in determining how to turn difficulties into possibility. For that reason, in the struggle for change, we must be neither solely patient nor solely impatient, but (as noted) patiently impatient. Unlimited patience, one that is never restless, ends up immobilizing transformative action. The same is the case with willful impatience, which demands immediate results from action even while it is still being planned.[17]

15. Moltmann, *Vida Esperança e Justiça*, 26 (translation mine).

16. Freire, *Pedagogy of Indignation*, 14.

17. Freire, *Pedagogy of Heart*, 64.

In the meantime, as we wait patiently impatient, we take comfort in the words of St. Augustine who declares, "Hope has two beautiful daughters; their names are Anger and Courage: Anger at the way things are, and Courage to see that they do not remain as they are."[18] Thus, in our quest to transform difficulties into possibilities and to wait patiently impatient, we hold fast to our hope, and allow ourselves the right to be angry about what we see and endure, and the courage to change what is needed.

Anger, as Donaldo Macedo argues,[19] is a tool that enables those who yearn for social justice to regain dignity without falling into cynicism. In addition, from a Freirean perspective, anger must be tempered with hope, as Nita Freire indicates in the Prologue of *Pedagogy of Indignation*. She affirms that hope " . . . is the very matrix for any dialectic between hope itself, anger or indignation, and love." Later she recapitulates Freire's words saying, " . . . we cannot forget . . . all truly ethical and genuinely human actions are born from two contradictory feelings, and only from two: love and anger."[20] Biblical prophets seemed to have known these feelings well. Their words are outbursts of fierce emotions to relentlessly rebuke the injustices perpetrated by evildoers while at the same time exhibiting a deep sensitivity toward human pain and suffering. What may be seen by many as normal events of life—exploitation, crimes, violence, hypocrisy—the prophets' eyes see as a threat to human welfare.

In their pursuit of justice, prophets offer a different interpretation of life events for those who practice injustices, and for those who are the victims of injustices. Being provoked by the problems and touched by the pain, prophets are taken by just rage and concerns for the dispossessed. In their quest to denounce the reality as seen, and announce what may come, prophets elicit the development of an alternative consciousness. Therefore, to hope against hope within dark times requires perseverance, resilience, and an alternative consciousness, which ultimately involves a learning process—a task redemptive communities need to embrace.

From a Freirean perspective, an alternative consciousness is the response to overcome situations that preclude people from their humanness. For Freire, these limit-situations are not " . . . the impassable boundaries where possibilities end, but the real boundaries where all possibilities

---

18. Brown, *Spirituality and Liberation*, 136.

19. Freire, *Pedagogy of Indignation*, xi.

20. Ibid., xxx.

begin."[21] Thus, a critical reading of the reality, which implies a learning process to confront the limit-situations, will unveil and direct critical actions toward achieving the untested feasibility implicit in that perception.[22] Through this process, people acquire the ability to intervene in reality as it unfolds and reveals. In addition, when people are able to live in the plenitude of the praxis—action and reflection—that is, when their actions encompass a critical reflection about their circumstances, they move from a purely naïve perception of reality to a critical awareness of it.[23] This process is what Freire calls conscientization or consciousness-raising,[24] which entails a dialectical relation between action and reflection, leading people to embrace their agency. This dynamic progression through which a person is able to analyze the concrete situation and gain an understanding of the roots, limits, and possibilities is vital and necessary to reach an accurate reading of reality that compels one to see the contradictions of life, reject them, and take a stand to overcome them. Accordingly, it cannot be considered a method or technique without connection to the social structure, nor can it be deemed an idealization of the praxis.

The process of transformation inherent to critical consciousness, to which Freire refers, demands a continued movement guided toward the transformation of social reality, without which the old patterns of perception will remain unchanged. Such cultural action, in which a person realizes his/her socio-cultural situation and overcomes his/her state of alienation and ingenuity, allows people to recognize themselves as conscious beings and co-creators of the future. For that reason, critical awareness happens not when there is a discourse about injustices, but indeed when actions, through praxis, are taken seriously to transform that reality. In being proactive, we are making " . . . an effort, humbly so, to narrow the distance between what we say and what we do as much as possible."[25] Truly, this is a lesson faith communities must learn. Reducing the distance between what is "preached" and what is "practiced" is a challenge to be accomplished, not only by preachers but by religious educators as well. Justice, dignity,

21. Freire, *Pedagogy of the Oppressed*, 80.

22. Ibid., 83–90.

23. Ibid., 112.

24. This word is a translation of the Portuguese word "conscientização," which was popularized by another Brazilian, the remarkable priest Dom Hélder Camara, who coined it during the process of creation of the Grassroots Education Movement in Brazil, 1961. It was later adapted and adopted by Freire.

25. Freire, *Pedagogy of Indignation*, 21.

ethical commitment, and compassion toward the needs of "the least of these" are not mere rhetorical elements to deliver in well-crafted teachings and appealing homilies. It does not suffice to learn how to read the "word of God," to develop a sound exegesis of the text, or even internalize and reproduce verses from the holy text, if the reading and its interpretation is not lived out, not embodied on a daily basis. When innocents are still being murdered, the widow, the elderly, and the poor have precarious means of survival, the foreigner is still discriminated against, radical hospitality and social justice are not shaping a faith community's ethos. What's worse, when that very community remains passive and silenced before such conditions that threaten human existence and dignity, the true meaning of education—transformation—has not been achieved.

Therefore, it is fundamental that faith communities equip people "to learn to read the world" if they wish to make a contribution to transform reality. As Freire proposes, we need to learn how to "read the world in order to be able to read the word."[26] This way of thinking brings the faith community face-to-face with its responsibility to promote a critical reading of our contexts, challenging the conventional ways of interpreting this reality—interpretations which many times have been undertaken with theologies that support ideologies that remain triumphalist and colonialist, or theologies that are *alienated* and *alienating* regarding the political, economic, and socio-cultural aspects of societies at large. The critical reading of the word of God should promote an emancipatory understanding of that word in connection with the present reality. As Tércio Junker emphasizes, " . . . the prophetic community has the potential to transform an old oppressive reality into a new redemptive experience of liberation . . . . As God's gift for the life of the world, the prophetic community is called to act with commitment against all signs of anti-life that compromise the dignity of humanity and the stability of the Creator order."[27] Faith communities aiming to become redemptive communities recognize the vital role they must incorporate in times such as the ones our societies are steeped in today.

Redemptive Communities

Considering the elements exposed above, it is important to highlight some of the pedagogical principles that will help faith communities in their quest

26. Freire and Macedo, *Literacy*, 35

27. Tércio Junker, *Prophetic Liturgy*, 136–137.

to become redemptive communities. For instance, in this journey of exploration, such communities need to recognize the role they play within society by not setting themselves apart from the socio-cultural context to which they belong. In light of that, they need to develop a collective critical consciousness so they will discern the best way to engage and participate in the life of the community and society. These elements, intrinsically related to what kind of educational vision the faith community will maintain, are important to delimit the ground of the pedagogy that should be employed.

As a discipline, pedagogy encompasses much more than methods and techniques. It refers to the educational phenomena in its multidimensional aspects: cultural, philosophical, psychological, biological, historical, and social. Thus, the sociopolitical and socio-historical dimensions of education—through which and from which one organizes the methodological actions necessary to contribute to human advancement—are significant aspects that a faith community needs in order to reflect on and put into action. As Henry Giroux maintains, pedagogy is a form of cultural production that implies the construction and organization of knowledge, desires, values, and social practices that should expand the principles of human dignity, liberty, and social justice.[28] Therefore, by observing the pedagogical practices of a community, it is possible to identify the embedded assumptions present in them—that is, if they have endorsed unequal and misogynist perspectives or if they have conversely fostered people's critical consciousness based on a liberating pedagogy.[29] The understanding of pedagogy from the perspective of liberation helps faith communities arrive at a dialogical understanding of what it means to educate in ways that embody hope and enhance our imagination.

Two of the characteristics of liberation pedagogy that Freire emphasizes are the role of "reading the world," and the importance of "dialogue" to build new foundations for conciliatory coexistence in society. In addition to these characteristics, it is important to stress Bruggemann's sense of the power of imagination to articulate new possibilities and realities. These elements should be part of our community as we seek to embody God's shalom—embodied redemption in its full stretch. Furthermore, as Brueggemann reiterates, faith communities can gain insights by paying close attention to the way poets and prophets conduct themselves. He is

28. Giroux, *Border Crossings*, 3–4.

29. For further discussion on 'pedagogy and "liberation pedagogy'" see: Débora B.A. Junker. "Beyond the Domestication of Pedagogy," 63.

convinced that poets and prophets "not only discerned the new actions of God that others did not discern, but they wrought the new actions of God by the power of their imagination, their tongues, their words. New poetic imagination evoked new realities in the community."[30]

The way poets and prophets embody God's action—through imagination, body, words—suggests a path to be embraced by faith communities. In the Bible as well as in our everyday lives, our hopes are nourished when a community decides to confront the injustices, the difficulties, and calamities of our context. The very act of confronting an undesired reality is a hope that something can and should be done to transform reality. We are often perplexed by the unpredictability of the world, the frightening escalation of violence, and the lack of compassion we witness in our everyday interactions. In spite of all these facts, we strongly long for actions of solidarity and justice, and for compassionate relationships to prevail. Like the prophets in the Bible, we seek to remember what could give us hope, and by remembering the events and gestures that bring us hope, we attempt to avoid personal and collective amnesia—which desensitizes people to the violence and suffering of this world.

Redemptive communities are sites of resistance conceived in hope. Moltmann reminds us of this when he states, "Within the risks of our time, the hope shows its strength, which comforts us and enables us to resist. Because of hope, we do not give up, but we remain as dissatisfied and restless beings living in an unfair and not redeemed world."[31] These communities know that the pain and struggles they face produce endurance, and endurance shapes an individual's and a community's character. Because they have learned and embodied Jesus' teachings, they are capable of applying his teachings in the concrete situations of their lives. Jesus is the embodiment of a resilient being. In his life, he encountered countless situations of pain, marginalization, and injustices. During his ministry, he confronted cultural prejudices, religious legalism, and the oppressive power of the Roman Empire. However, he resisted them by providing an alternative consciousness to those with whom he met. His commitment to meet the needs of "the least of these" was embodied in his attitudes, in his words, and in his deeds. Resistance in Jesus' life could be translated as subversive because in such a context of material, religious, and ethical deprivation, he offered alternative ways of imagining and being in this world that were in direct contrast with

---

30. Brueggemann, *Hopeful Imagination*, 2.

31. Moltmann, *Vida Esperança e Justiça*, 25 (translation mine).

the established order. He fed the hungry; he healed the sick; he showed acts of justice and compassion toward the needy. He also rebuked those who despised and oppressed the poor. As Jack Seymour insightfully reminds us, "The redemptive community rooted in the surprising graciousness of God was at the heart of the Jesus movement—where people and systems were humanized and where the excluded found a place of welcome and inclusion."[32] Furthermore, when communities embody Jesus' teaching, their lives radiate what Seymour calls signs of redemptive community: forgiveness, hope, redemption, love, and justice. Hence, redemptive communities have the task to be firmly anchored in a thoughtful and coherent understanding of the message of the gospel, committed to the people as Jesus was.

Redemptive communities have the responsibility to promote a critical reading of reality seeking to understand it from the perspective of excluded groups, that is, in opposition to the dominant interpretation of a particular reality. This critical reading will undoubtedly unveil discriminatory acts and denounce unjust arrangements. Redemptive communities are original in their ways of living out hope. They cannot become fixed entities dictating to others what they need to do, or be, in order to gain a critical consciousness, because their critical interpretations of reality are born out of their own context of struggle and their engagement with their circumstances.

Redemptive communities are also sites of protest against all that diminishes us as human beings. For that reason, they are risky sites in which to live, but also fertile fields to thrive. They know that their presence in the world is not without risks, and is not neutral either. Redemptive communities recognize that history is impregnated with possibilities and hope. However, to make that possibility tangible, we must actively engage and intervene in the world. Redemptive communities are places to nurture and hold each other accountable in the struggle for justice. The fight for justice should, indeed, be manifested through vigils, protests, and civil disobedience as it exposes the many forms of veiled violence that take place in the silence of cathedrals, in the hidden recesses of streets corners, and in the private spheres of society. Exercising a collective consciousness should lead the community to the rejection of conveniently silencing itself when it faces systemic prejudices or when terrorism is retaliated with terrorism. Such a community should not accept when bible verses are used and misused to justify self-interest, or when there are concerns about the poor and hungry

32. Seymour, *Teaching the Way of Jesus*, 164.

overseas, but the poor and undernourished in the neighborhood next door are left untouched. They should speak up when selective aspects of liberation movements are opportunely dismissed or ignored, allowing the very structures that create human misery to remain unchallenged. Surely, redemptive communities are bound to be imperfect spaces; however, it is their duty to continue to imaginatively seek to embody God's love and compassion.

Through their collective consciousness they should be able to analyze where they have failed and seek out ways to overcome their shortcomings by doing justice, practicing loving kindness, and by walking humbly with God and God's people (Micah 6:8). In spite of the daunting challenges that these educational principles entail, we should not be discouraged from emboldening faith communities to embrace a critical consciousness as they participate in the construction of a world grounded in the teachings of a compassionate God. Thus, faith communities should become a locus of resilient hope. Out of the dark places of our context narratives of hope flourish out of solidarity. In this sense, redemptive communities are channels through which God's vision inspires and propels people to speak on God's behalf, sharpening our vision, challenging our imagination, and modifying our actions. Redemptive communities are places where human creativity and responsibility walk together to construct channels of exchange between those who have and those who do not. They work in solidarity toward transformative relationships. Redemptive communities do not silence their prophets; on the contrary, they nurture them, care about them, and learn from them. In fact, in the process of learning from each other, the redemptive community becomes a prophetic community. Ultimately, redemptive communities—when living the full potential of *prophetic* praxis—are the light that illumines the paths of the hopeless, open the airways of those who cry "I can't breathe," provide shelter for those who have been enslaved by the economic systems, and imagine ways together in which dignity and divine love can be experienced. Redemptive communities are spaces pregnant with the possibility of sharing experiences, of weaving new narratives, a space for communion, for dialogue, for cooperative work, for inclusion, and for learning as a process of change—the visible anticipation of God's peaceable kin-dom.

Conclusion.

> Is not this the fast that I choose: to loose the bonds of injustice, to
> undo the thongs of the yoke, to let the oppressed go free, and to
> break every yoke? Is it not to share your bread with the hungry,
> and bring the homeless poor into your house; when you see the
> naked, to cover them, and not to hide yourself from your own
> kin? Then your light shall break forth like the dawn, and your heal-
> ing shall spring up quickly; your vindicator shall go before you, the
> glory of the Lord shall be your rearguard. Then you shall call, and
> the Lord will answer; you shall cry for help, and he will say, Here
> I am (Is 58:6–9).

Human journey is a risky and faulty enterprise full of contradictions. It
is also a venture full of possibilities. When human pathos encounters the
divine ethos, a space is opened that enables human agency to flourish
through solidary works that favor the common good. As mentioned previously in this chapter, when hope is not paralyzed in the attempt to escape
from the world and rather finds itself engaged and committed to alleviating
life's struggles, it constitutes a fire that is able to ignite, to inspire, and to give
glimmers of what is not yet realized but is soon to be accomplished.

In times of trouble and trials, we find refuge in poetry because words
and images do not only feed our intellect, but speak to our hearts and souls.
When our minds cannot process or bear all the hope-less atrocities, and
when our eyes cannot see and our ears cannot hear, we search our hearts
and wonder about other possibilities. As members of redemptive communities—and as people who embody the hope of God—we cannot wait
in silence in dark places for the realities to resolve themselves and for the
struggles to subside so we can finally see the light. Instead, we need to be
conscious of where we are "in the darkness" while being mindful "of the
light." This means that we must acquire a conscience of location and a conscience of destination. Although we may find ourselves asking for a map,
a recipe, or a set of instructions that will take us from our current location
into a new destination, each of our communities is created uniquely and,
thus, a single set of maps, "one size fits all," would prove faulty and mis-
leading. From a Freirean perspective, this is precisely where the challenge
is located—in the intersection of conscience of what is and the imagining
of what can be.

We must, then, foster opportunities for reflection within our own communities that will allow us to look at our own realities and be challenged to

transform by means of our own agencies. We must roll up our sleeves and believe that the present reality can be overcome one day. That is what hope fosters in us. Our hope is based in our call to conscience, in our solidarity, in our political will to change, in our participation as citizens and our identity as Christians. Out of hope, we confront the adversities, the injustices, the need and the call to change. In the articulation of our arguments and analysis of our contexts, we carry on the seeds of change. Authentic biblical hope emerges when we are able to embody the divine compassion towards the suffering places of the world, illuminating the future with the "torch of hope."[33] That torch will lead us in our hope-filled journey, as German-born political theorist Hannah Arendt wonderfully and poetically summarized:

> Even in the darkest of times we have the right to expect some illumination, and such illumination may well come less from theories and concepts than from the uncertain, flickering, and often weak light that some men and women, in their lives and their works, will kindle under almost all circumstances and shed over the time span that was given them on earth.[34]

Perhaps this is the time to hear the voices of those who come from the suffering corners of the earth. Perhaps this is the time to follow them—for they bear the torch of hope—so that they may illumine our way leading us into the possibility of becoming an embodied redemptive community.

Bibliography

Arendt, Hannah. *Men in Dark Times*. New York: Harcourt Brace, 1968, ix.

Brown, Robert McAfee. *Spirituality and Liberation: Overcoming the Great Fallacy*. Philadelphia: Westminster, 1988.

Brueggemann, Walter. *Hopeful Imagination: Prophetic Voices in Exile*. Philadelphia: Fortress,1986.

———, *The Prophetic Imagination*. 2nd Edition. Minneapolis: Fortress, 2001.

Croatto, Severino. "Composición y Querigma del Libro de Isaias," in *RIBLA*, n. 35/36, 2000.

Freire, Paulo. *Pedagogy of Heart*. New York: Continuum, 1998.

———, *Pedagogy of Hope*. New York: Continuum, 2007.

———, *Pedagogy of Indignation*. Boulder, CO: Paradigm, 2004.

Freire, Paulo and Donaldo Macedo. *Literacy: Reading the Word & the World*. South Hadley, MA: Bergin & Garvey, 1987.

---

33. Moltmann, *Vida Esperança e Justiça*, 23 (translation mine).

34. Arendt, *Men in Dark Times*, ix.

Giroux, Henry A. *Border Crossings: Cultural Workers and the Politics of Education.* New York: Routledge, 1992.

Heschel, Abraham. *The Prophets: An Introduction.* Vol.1. New York: Harper & Row, 1962.

———, *The Prophets.* Vol.2. New York: Harper & Row, 1962.

Isasi-Diaz, Ada Maria and Yolanda Tarango. *Hispanic Women: Prophetic Voice in the Church.* Minneapolis: Fortress, 1992.

Junker, Débora B.A. "Beyond the Domestication of Pedagogy: Envisioning New Perspectives on Education." *Encounter* 74.3 (2014) 45-65.

Junker, Tércio. *Prophetic Liturgy: Toward a Transforming Christian Praxis.* Eugene, Oregon: Pickwick, 2014.

Moltmann, Jürgen. *The Power of the Powerless: The Word of Liberation for Today.* San Francisco: Harper & Row, 1982.

———. *Vida Esperança e Justiça: Um Testamento Teológico para a América Latina.* EDITEO: São Bernardo do Campo, 2008.

Parker, Evelyn. *Trouble Don't Last Always: Emancipatory Hope Among African American Adolescents.* Cleveland: Pilgrim, 2003.

Seymour, Jack L. *Teaching the Way of Jesus: Educating Christians for Faithful Living,* Nashville: Abingdon, 2014.

Stanley, Christopher D. *The Hebrew Bible: A Comparative Approach.* Minneapolis: Fortress, 2010.

6

Communicability,
Redeemability, Educability

——— *Mai-Anh Le Tran* ———

Know Your Neighbor...

"MY NAME IS MAI-ANH, but you can call me '*Kumi Na Saba*.'" The group roared with laughter. It was the first meeting of 14 wide-eyed students and three faculty/staff of Eden Theological Seminary in St. Louis, Missouri, and students and faculty of our host institution, the Reformed Institute for Theological Training (RITT) in Eldoret, Kenya. The Eden students recognized the coded appellation. The Kenyan students, on the other hand, wondered whether they should politely tell me that perhaps I had misspoken Kiswahili. "*Kumi na saba* is Swahili for the number 17...do you know that?" the Dean of RITT said, grinning ear to ear. I proceeded to explain: Since it was so hard to keep track of us band of seventeen travelers, I had proposed that we assign each person a number, one to seventeen, for easy count-off each time we gather. My faculty colleague was #1, and I was #17. "Oh!" More laughter ensued.

We continued with the game "Know Your Neighbor," with rounds of introductions for that morning's first joint study session at RITT. Facilitated by the dry-witted "Rev. Dean," we said the names of persons to our left and right, a fun ritual signaling the beginning of new friendships. "My name is Manuel," my seat neighbor proceeded, "to my right is Annette, and to my left is Prof. Kumi Na Saba." Such was the initiation of a new form of community....

Postcolonial (Tres)Passings

For two weeks in January of 2014, I accompanied the students and faculty of this seminary-sponsored travel study seminar to Kenya. The group traveled from Nairobi to Eldoret and Turkana. I was with them only for activities in Nairobi and Eldoret, and then lingered in the capital city for one week on my own. It was my very first time to set foot upon African soil, and the journey required nothing short of step-by-step learning, relearning, and unlearning.

Three days after our arrival in the country, a terrorist attempt involving IEDs (improvised explosive devices) took place at Jomo Kenyatta International Airport. Security scans were routine at every entrance to just about every major public venue, including shopping malls, university libraries, and churches. Guards armed with rifles screened my bag as I entered a large church in an upper/middle-class neighborhood of Nairobi for worship on the last Sunday of January. Once inside, I heard lively contemporary Christian praise music, and earnest prayers that God's faithful people would "soak in His [sic] love, majesty, and graciousness."

Visiting the University of Nairobi, I innocently asked for a campus map, and a staff member replied, "You are asking for very critical information. A terrorist could come and ask for a map of our campus!" She chuckled wryly, but she was only half joking. A day in the university's libraries afforded me opportunities to thumb through the writings of Kenyan scholars such as John S. Mbiti and Jesse N.K. Mugami on the colonization and Christianization of East Africa; to skim Masters theses on the 2007 postelection violence and its impact on women in camps for IDPs (internally displaced persons); and to peruse national syllabi for "Christian religious education," a standardized subject matter for both public and sectarian (religious) primary and secondary schools.

In the meanwhile, the seminary students of the Global North underwent experiences unparalleled to anything that had ever encountered in their lives: long, exhausting, roller-coaster bus rides; outdoor latrines that require incredible thigh muscles and nimble limbs, *lots* of hand sanitizers, and the willingness to be soiled; church meals consisting of rice, beans, cabbage, prepared "in the wild" and in the presence of (with some participation by) sprightly livestock. They made new friends, played dominoes, washed their own clothes by hand, wiped down bodies when there is no water, showered in brisk cold temperatures when water heaters do not work, maneuvered mosquito nets, read, journaled, painted, talked, laughed, fought, cried, recoiled, reconciled, asked questions, jumped to conclusions, revised their conclusions, and just began to learn how to ask open questions.

For two weeks, we magi of the West traversed lands to which we do not belong. Thanks to introductory postcolonial lessons, we at least learned that not everything we see and touch is ours. We made risky contacts— risky for us and for our hospitable guests. In the process, we had to *relearn* what it means to eat, to pray, and to love as human beings bound by *community* and *communicability*. In a country where barbwires make average household fences, security guards march about with weapons as though they were toy guns, a camera inopportunely displayed might get you into trouble, the Bible is the canon for proper Christian social, cultural, and ethical behaviors, and the incumbent President had once appeared before the International Criminal Court for "crimes against humanity"[1] (for activities during the country's violent 2007 election), one has to rethink assumptions of security and insecurity, of what saves and what kills.

Educating in/for Redemptive Community

The vignettes above reflect both the fertility and fragility of our *chronos* time. Religions teach love of neighbor, but reality reminds us repeatedly that it is hard to know who is neighbor and who is enemy—in many times and places, we are both neighbor and enemy to one another. Despite forecasts about rising secularism and post-religious, post-Christian movements in North America, we have empirical descriptions of exploding charismatic spiritualities and the swelling of new "Christendoms" in the Global South.[2] The transnational flows of peoples have collapsed contexts, but have also exposed the fierce reflexes of physical and social immune systems triggered by risky human contact. Opportunities to share meals, fellowship, and prayers with new friends across the globe remind us of the early Christian communities' seemingly ideal habits (Acts 2:42). But the allergies and pathogens—biological and social—encountered during border-crossings also remind us of how these basic human activities of eating, praying, and loving challenge our notions of what is "redemptive" and what

---

1. Karimi, "Kenyan President Uhuru Kenyatta at ICC over Changes Linked to 2007 Violence," CNN, http://www.cnn.com/2014/10/08/world/africa/kenya-icc-status-hearing/.

2. Jenkins, *The Next Christendom*.

is "community." Every now and then, standing in liminal, *chronos* time, we gasp for realized-hope, because "we can't breathe."

Attending to such moments, scholars-practitioners of religious education ask: what does it mean to teach for *faith* in such a time as this? What does it mean to have faith *in* a world that is so volatile and virulent? The critical pedagogist Henry Giroux argues that we live in a conjuncture in which the public pedagogies of socio-cultural, socio-political "*dis*imagination machines" strip away our capacities to "become critically engaged citizens of the world."[3] For Giroux, such capacities include the ability to calibrate one's moral conscience, a sense of social agency, the ability to engage in structural analysis, the skills of self-reflective dialogue, and the courage for passionate action, and a robust imagination about the collective good.[4] If these vital capacities are being chipped away, then what resources of critical education and critical faith might we call upon to restore them to vibrant use?

This chapter attempts the above meta-questions by tuning attention to the three operative words found in the title of this anthology: educating, redemptive, community. They yield three simpler questions: What does it mean to educate? What does it mean to redeem? What does it mean to be community? Let us take these questions in *reverse* order.

Communicability

Dorothy Bass, in a 1995 essay with religious educators Mary Boys and Sara Lee, points to an enduring issue for Protestant Christian education in the later part of the twentieth-century. It is "the conflation of the priesthood of all believers with secular or civil religious forms of individualism."[5] A burst of renewing energy of the Reformation era, the priesthood of all believers was a theological conviction that motivated lay Christians "to take seriously their own calling to study, to serve, and even to lead as members of the Body of Christ."[6] However, over the years, the social, cultural, and economic landscape of the U.S. has become one in which religion is re-

---

3. Giroux, *The Violence of Organized Forgetting*, 26–27.

4. Ibid., 82–83.

5. Boys, et. al., "Protestant, Catholic, Jew," 268. The second major issue for Bass is Protestantism's interfaith struggle and its inability to sustain public Christian identity outside of presumed cultural dominance.

6. Ibid.

duced to "a private, individual matter," and "life habits" are nurtured based on "consumerism and autonomy." Bass states: "[T]he Reformation heritage of individual freedom for ministry has become confused with American ideals of individual freedom from obligation . . . . Belonging and believing are seen as matters of personal choice, and it is difficult to sustain communities within which growth in faith can be nurtured."[7] "Life habits" are nurtured in such a way that we have confused "freedom for ministry" with "freedom from communal responsibility." Boyung Lee puts it bluntly in her book, *Transforming Congregations through Community*: "sometimes, what the church calls 'community' is really only a 'gathering of individuals in reciprocal relationships,' who will opt-out of the collective when things are no longer interesting, or demands of the group become too burdensome."[8] It is an interesting irony: We love the idea of community, we exhort one another to "build community," and yet we have a hard time figuring out why it is hard to *be* in community, and we struggle to admit that sometimes being in community hurts us.

Epidemiology—the study of communicable diseases—provides an interesting way to unpack this quagmire. Community requires human contact, and we live in a world in which community is configured by communicability.[9]

"Communicability Configuring Community"

It is eerie how the fatal shooting of 18-year-old Michael Brown in Ferguson and the resurgence of the Ebola virus occurred in the U.S. in striking time parallel. We have two individuals—Mr. Michael Brown and Mr. Thomas Eric Duncan—who succumbed to entwining systems of "infectious diseases," in which, ironically, they both were configured in public imagination as threatening pollutants. In micro-biological terms, Thomas Duncan, a Liberian national, was the carrier who brought the Ebola virus into the United States, and thereby infected two nurses from within the country's borders before his death on October 8, 2014. However, Mr. Duncan also died a social death, in which a virus of fear in public imagination turned him into a "foreign contagion" that invaded the borders, safety, security, and well-being of what is supposed to be an untouchable, impenetrable nation.

7. Ibid., 268–69.

8. Lee, *Transforming Congregations Through Community*, 14–15.

9. Wald, *Contagious*, 12.

This same virus of fear also struck down the marked body of Michael Brown, as it ruthlessly strikes a host of *Otherly* marked bodies: racialized bodies, sexualized bodies, the transient bodies of those homeless, LGBTQ bodies, the "alien" bodies of undocumented immigrants. A fear-stricken social imagination deems them dangerous upon contact: we must not let them near; we must quarantine them; we must disinfect ourselves of them; they will hurt us or deplete our systems; if they touch us, we will die!

In her fascinating book, *Contagious*,[10] professor of English, Priscilla Wald breaks down the scripts of outbreak narratives in scientific and popular literature since the discovery of the first known "chronic typhoid germ distributor" in 1907—the first "human carrier," popularly known as "Typhoid Mary." Analyzing depictions and discussions of Cold War epidemics, HIV/AIDS, the initial discovery of Ebola, to SARS, Wald sketches how "epidemiology dramatizes human beings' mortal struggle with their environment, social and biological."[11]

According to Wald, whether it is in our attempts to understand microbes or social relations, human beings are "plagued" by the *Other* as we grapple with the paradox: human intercourse binds us together, but it also makes us sick.[12] Contagion literally means "to touch together," and was first used in the fourteenth century to refer to the "circulation of ideas and attitudes," often with a connotation of social and moral "danger or corruption."[13] As industrialization facilitated urban constructions of community, "[t]he growth of cities gave rise to what [was considered to be] 'promiscuous' social spaces: people literally and figuratively bumping up against each other in smaller spaces and larger numbers than ever before."[14]

"Communicable diseases" (the original first two words for the acronym CDC) have biological and moral dimensions. The spread of disease exposes human ignorance, vulnerability, and promiscuity. Human carriers easily become scapegoats: they are "examples of the transgressions of the group for which they symbolically suffered."[15] Epidemics justify "regulation with 'terrifying urgency,'" and they set in motion "'the administrative machinery for disease prevention, sanitary super-vision, and, in general, protection of

10. Ibid.
11. Ibid., 21.
12. Ibid., 2.
13. Ibid., 12.
14. Ibid., 14.
15. Ibid., 17.

community health."[16] "Quarantine" and "surveillance" become two crucial strategies for containment of disease—and in the age of transnationalism, "global surveillance" is justified not only for reasons of "national defense," but also as a matter of "national public health."[17] An infection/infestation is an invasion of the body—physical and national.

"Community of the Age of Salvation"

A community of faith is configured by the fundamental activities of eating, praying, and loving. The messiness of these practices when performed in communal settings is perhaps a reflection of our cultural assumption that these are private life habits of autonomous individuals. We assume idealistically that *eating* first and foremost belongs to the arena of home and hearth, in such sanitized and stocked settings as kitchens and dining rooms, until we factor in the economics of "eating out," and the politics of the food, advertising, production, manufacturing, and service industries which make possible or impossible our abilities to eat—even eat around dinner tables—on a daily basis. We assume that *loving* also is a "personal thing"—the arenas for which are largely hidden spaces, whether or not permissible (from the bedroom to public parks), until we factor in the public morality plays, and socio-cultural and legislative regulations of "how" and "whom" to love. We also assume that "praying" belongs to self-select private or sectarian domains, until we are reminded by liturgical theologians such as Marjorie Proctor-Smith that praying is a very "political act," and that sometimes death-dealing "community" can render us silent—unable and unwilling to pray.[18]

From this angle, we see how the prayer that Jesus taught his disciples offered a new imagination on how to pray, how to eat, and how to love. Crafted for a band of followers who already knew how to pray in private devotion and public worship, the Jesus prayer (Luke 11:2–4; Matt 6:9–13) was an Aramaic prayer, taught for vernacular tongues, the words and form of which echo the ancient Jewish prayer *Kaddish*.[19] The distinction, argues Joachim Jeremias, lies in how each petition of the Jesus prayer leans into an

16. Ibid.

17. Ibid., 25.

18. Smith, *Praying with Our Eyes Open*, 10.

19. Jeremias, *The Prayers of Jesus*, 76, 93, 98.

"eschatology becoming actualized."[20] It is "a brief summary of the fundamentals of Jesus' proclamation" about the saving work that God has already begun.[21] Joachim Jeremias's exposition helps make this point:

> Jesus' disciples recognized themselves as a community, or more exactly as the *community of the age of salvation*, and . . . they requested of Jesus a prayer which would bind them together and identify them, in that it would bring to expression their chief concern.[22]

One could say that the prayer Jesus taught de-privatized and de-individualized the urgent concerns of daily life, and makes inseparable matters of earth and heaven, for in the realm of God, "earthly things [are] hallowed."[23] Thus, the "community of the age of salvation"— a community that actively realizes with God wholeness and fullness of all life—is one that imagines:

- Abundant life through practices of eating and drinking,
- Forgiveness of the cycles of debts,
- Preservation in times of trials and tribulations,
- Repentance from violent "allergies" to one another,
- Human contact is hallowed contact,
- for God's kin(g)dom has come, and earthly things are hallowed.

A question arises for the tasks of Christian religious education: How are we honest and educative about the risks and potentialities of human community and human communicability?

Redeemability

According to Priscilla Wald, responses to epidemics do not just reveal human fear and misgivings about contact. They also reveal some positive aspects of human community: that we are inextricably interdependent; we are resilient and resourceful in efforts toward healing; and we believe that "healing" is spiritual, even when we are dealing with biological diseases. The last point is particularly instructive: While there is always a mystifying

20. Ibid., 107.
21. Ibid., 77, 99, 107.
22. Ibid., 94. Italics added.
23. Ibid., 101.

"superstitious" dimension to human apprehensions about diseases—sometimes in defiance of clear science, often driven by ignorance—but there is also a fierce respect for what Wald calls "medical and religious rituals"[24] in our efforts toward healing.

"The Human Being is a repairing animal," writes philosopher Elizabeth V. Spelman in her book, *Repair: The Impulse to Restore in a Fragile World*.[25] The repair work ranges from mechanical to medical, relational to social, psychological to environmental; and the brokenness, decay, or destruction that compel mending can be consequences of everyday wear and tear, or violent "deliberate destruction" that leaves "ruins."[26] The repair words in the English vocabulary are illuminating: "renewal, redemption, reconciliation, salvation, compensation, consolation, resilience, restoration, repair; to heal, mend, recover, rebuild, resolve, reconstruct."[27] Lodging repair "at the very heart of justice,"[28] Spelman discusses the range of restorative options with case studies of historic injuries. She makes an interesting assertion about the ethic of care in the work of repair: "the moral agent as problem solver," or repairer, has "intimate knowledge of the parts [they deal] with—intimate both in the sense of having or seeking specific and nuanced and contextualized knowledge of the people involved and the situations they are in, and in the sense of acknowledging or creating a close relationship to the people involved."[29]

The Christian faith community has a "religious ritual" for this kind of repair work that brings intimacy of knowledge and intimacy of relationship among people standing in the midst of ruins. We call this ritual *prayer*.

Persistent Pursuit

When confronted with messy community and dangerous communicability, faith communities fervently resort to prayer as one of those "life habits" (to echo the words of Dorothy Bass) that preserves and restores hope. Nina Pham—the first nurse who contracted the Ebola virus from Thomas Duncan—is profiled on the Internet as being very religious. Her family belongs

24. Wald, *Contagious*, 17.
25. Spelman, *Repair*, 1.
26. Ibid., 103, 105.
27. Ibid., 121.
28. Ibid., 51.
29. Ibid., 47.

to a Catholic parish in Fort Worth, and during her illness they claimed hope through the power of prayer. When Thomas Duncan died, his family said he is now in the hands of God. In St. Louis and beyond, religious folk pray for "justice for Michael Brown."

What is "prayer," in light of the human impulse to repair?

John Shelby Spong draws a distinction between "praying" and "saying prayers" in his book, *Honest Prayer*.[30] In the book, the revered theologian admits that he struggles with prayer: he is "drawn" by its power, and yet "repelled" by its forms.[31] Along with a host of other theologians and mystics, Spong reminds us that "prayer" is not what one *says*: "prayer" is what one *does*. So, as prayer is traditionally understood as "a human attempt to make contact with God,"[32] for Spong, God is not somewhere out there or up there in the nebulous skies. God is "found *in* life, not *beyond* life,"[33] and therefore prayer is most fundamentally an attempt to open oneself to the transcendent and the holy as we face into this world. Theologian Douglas John Hall puts it this way: prayer is "thinking [and we might add, acting] your way into God's world."[34] The late religious educator Maria Harris put it in curricular terms: "prayer" is "a characteristic set of forms for addressing the mystery of God"; prayer fosters "*our way of being in the world before God*,"[35] a spirituality of deep communion with God and the world. In this deep attunement, we do what liturgical theologian Marjorie Procter-Smith insists upon: we pray with our "eyes wide open" to the "patterns of domination," to "resist in order to transform, to recreate the church as communal, sociable, healthy."[36]

The clergy and faith-based activists of Ferguson and St. Louis nailed this when they picked up the mantra attributed to Rabbi Abraham Heschel: "Praying with our Feet."[37]

The Bible is replete with stories of people "praying with their feet." Religious educator Thomas Groome lifts up one familiar tale: the parable of

---

30. Spong, *Honest Prayer*.

31. Ibid., 15.

32. Ibid., 29.

33. Ibid. Italics in text.

34. Hall, *When You Pray*.

35. Harris, *Fashion Me a People*, 94, 103.

36. Procter-Smith, *Praying with Our Eyes Open*, 14.

37. http://www.prayingwithourfeet.org. Accessed January 14, 2015.

"persistent widow" (Luke 18:1–8).[38] In this story, the exemplar of faith is a powerless widow who is annoyingly incessant in her demands for justice, so much that the judge—who is said to have no fear or respect for God or any other—finally has to give in. The New Interpreter's Study Bible points out a closer translation that shows the outrageous nature of this widow's persistence: "I will grant her justice," says the judge, "so that she may not finally come and slap me in the face" (18:6)!

Refusing to accept what unjust systems dictate as her fate, relentless in the pursuit of a corrective response, she is the example of what it means to pray, a reminder that prayer is an active pursuit of reparation, a model of how tenacious faith is a verb and not a noun. Concluding the parable, Jesus ruminates: at the end of the day, at the end of time, will there be faith like this on earth (18:8)?

Redemptive Difference

If the prayer of Jesus is illuminating for our understanding of community and communicability, then Jesus' parable of the persistent widow adds to our musings on redeemability. An evocative book by theologian David Kelsey is helpful here. In *Imagining Redemption*, Kelsey frames the question that Christians may ask when standing in the thick of what Spelman describes as ruins: "*What earthly difference can Jesus make here?*"[39] Expounding on foundational theological understandings of "redemption," Kelsey proposes three meanings that express what Christians believe to be the work of God in the "human scene,"[40] and as manifested in the life and ministry of Jesus: "(1) making up for a bad performance, (2) redeeming from alien control, and (3) making good on a promise."[41] Redemption is God's work of "[making up] for the world's bad performances"; it is God's work of relieving, bailing, extracting, freeing "persons and situations from oppressive powers that bind and distort them"; it is God's fulfillment of promises made to humankind, when the world fails to deliver.[42]

Jesus' persistent widow—and, one could say, Jesus himself—reflect tenacious faith in the reparability and redeemability of unjust situations and

---

38. Groome, *Will There Be Faith?*, 1.

39. Kelsey, *Imagining Redemption*, 6.

40. Ibid., 16.

41. Ibid.

42. Ibid., 17-19.

systems. We could implicate the church and religious leadership in Kelsey's redemptive formula and ask: What would it take to recalibrate the bad performances of communities of faith? What would it take to free communities of faith from the bondage of repressive, oppressive values, visions, and volitions? What would it take to make good on the faith community's failed promise—the promise of participating with God in repairing the world?[43]

A question arises for the tasks of Christian religious education: How do we teach toward the widow's exemplary faith—one that demands delivery of promises, correction of unjust performances by leadership, and release from death-dealing bondage?

This question leads us to *educability*.

Educability

We are told that Christian religious education is a communal enterprise of "drawing out"; the "artistic work" of creating, re-creating, fashioning, and refashioning communal life of faith for people "pledging their troth" to one another in covenants of love.[44] Put succinctly by Jack Seymour:

> Christian education must provide open spaces where people can learn the faith tradition, engage that tradition with issues of life, and seek to live together in ways that are faithful to God . . . . Through Christian education we face into the world, explore the deepest meanings of our lives, engage one another, and partner with a God seeking wholeness and meaning for all life.[45]

With the instincts for intimate knowledge and intimate relationship that Spelman's repairer would exude, Seymour and Margaret Ann Crain describe what it means to educate Christians at the intersection of meaning, learning, and vocation:

> While the *goal* of Christian religious education is to incarnate wholeness and justice, the process begins as religious educators seek to create hospitable and just spaces in which to practice God's presence. We *invite* others, by our very "being," into the process

43. Moore, *Teaching as a Sacramental Act*, 199–200. In Mary Elizabeth Moore's hermeneutics of sacramental teaching, the educational practices of reconstruction and repair follow God's "prophetic redemption"—"God's pull on a broken world toward wholeness—toward New Creation."

44. Harris, *Fashion Me a People*, 40–41.

45. Seymour, *Mapping Christian Education*, 118, 121.

of meaning-making. More than being mere role models, we too inhabit that space; we do not stand above or outside the space. Meaning-making profoundly focuses us on our own struggles for meaning, as well as on the construction projects of others. We are vulnerable. We must be *authentic*. Incarnational religious education may require simpler structures, but it asks more of the educator. We are fragile together and searching together to embody the call of God for justice in all creation.[46]

In Seymour and Crain's articulation, the previously described characteristics of communicability and redeemability are echoed: vulnerable struggle, invitational presence, fragile searching, focused, self-baring pursuit of meaning, wholeness, and justice. Their vision for the enterprise of Christian religious education invites members of redemptive communities to "face into the world" as creative, generative, repairing agents, who—to employ Spelman's repair words—educate toward *renewal* of moral conscience, *restoration* of communal agency, *reconstruction* of critical analysis, *resilience* in self-reflective dialogue, and *reconciliation* through passionate action.

Public theologian Harvey Cox convinces us that we live in the "age of the Spirit."[47] In this age, faith is awe, faith is wonder, faith is a conscious hope and confidence in God's in-breaking. Religions that facilitate such faith do not offer dogma; instead, they offer narratives that help people make meaning, rituals to intensify human experiences, and ethical guides for daily living. In this age of the Spirit, a faith community is redemptive when it makes good on performances and promises that the world *and* the church fail to deliver. In this age of the Spirit, a faith community is redemptive when it teaches people—through the curricula[48] of eating, praying, and loving—how to "set their hearts"[49] on repairing the broken situations and systems of the world.

"World Turned Upside Down"

Every religious educator aspires to educate toward transformation—after all, who would want to teach toward stasis? However, we also need to reckon

---

46. Seymour, et.al., *Educating Christians*, 188. Italics in text.

47. Cox, *The Future of Faith*.

48. "Curriculum" employed in the meaning of Maria Harris, as the "course of the church's life." Harris, *Fashion Me a People*, 63.

49. Little, *To Set One's Heart*.

with the potentialities of "transformation": it is both promising and threatening. In our zeal to transform, we forget that some ruins are irreparable and irredeemable, as Spelman points out.[50] Moreover, what is to distinguish the power of renewing transformation from power of destructive change?

In *The Christian Imagination*, theologian Willie James Jennings writes of the Andean notion of *pachacuti*, which means "world turned around" or "world turned upside down."[51] *Pachacuti* was the native Andean's term to refer to the epoch-turning arrival of the Spanish, who brought to the New World "Old World pathogens": "smallpox, influenza, tuberculosis, measles, and other diseases . . . ."[52] It is a familiar story of cultures collapsing and imaginations fossilizing under colonial contact. When lives like those of Michael Brown and Thomas Duncan are extinguished in ominous physical and social death, we wonder how resurrection is possible.

However, with tenacious faith, we follow Jennings's imagination and look back to the origin of that idyllic community that ate, prayed, and loved in Acts 2, an origin located in an explosive, uncontainable in-breaking of the Spirit. Jennings words are potent:

> If a world caught in the unrelenting exchange system of violence was to be overcome, then here was the very means God would use to overcome violence—by the introduction of a new reality of belonging that drew together different peoples into a way of life that intercepted ancient bonds and redrew them around the body of Jesus and in the power of the Spirit.[53]

Here, Jennings draws us to the redemptive power of the Spirit, which reconfigures community around a new space of intimate knowledge and intimate relationships, the center of which is the body of Jesus—a body resurrected and "vindicated"[54] against repressive human lordships, a body that proclaimed the rule of God on this earth in the here-and-now. In this new redemptive space, the human calculus of who is significant, who is image of God, who is pathogen or contagion, is turned upside down. In this space, the redemptive communicability of the Spirit reconfigures fragile human community.

---

50. Spelman, *Repair*, 102.

51. Jennings, *The Christian Imagination*, Kindle Locations 1603–4.

52. Ibid., Kindle Locations 1613.

53. Ibid., Kindle Locations 5940–42.

54. Seymour, *Teaching the Way of Jesus*, 157.

To educate for faith in this redemptive space is to teach as Jesus taught, Seymour insists. Jesus taught love for God and neighbor; he reminded people of God's graciousness; he pointed to the realm of God breaking into *chronos* time; his pedagogies of eating and drinking affirmed abundant life for all; he resisted in times of insidious trial. In proclaiming Jesus as "Resurrected One," we teach with tenacious conviction that from the ruins of death, God restores life.[55]

Touched

Anyone who has traveled internationally, especially to an "underdeveloped"[56] country like Kenya, knows full well the rituals of vaccinations—measures that safeguard personal, collective, and national security. The amount of sanitizing products that we packed for that short visit to Kenya reveals the absurdity of our fear of contamination. Along the way, we learned this truth: as physical immune systems toughened, social, emotional, and theological immune systems loosened. In eating together, praying for one another, and learning from each other, we cross-contaminated one another's ideas about church, world, God, and the meaning of theological vocation. We were learning in redemptive communities configured by the infectious Spirit. We were learning to eat, pray, and love in the way of Jesus.

Bibliography

Boys, Mary C., Sara S. Lee, and Dorothy C. Bass. "Protestant, Catholic, Jew: The Transformative Possibilities of Educating Across Religious Boundaries." *Religious Education* 90:2 (1995) 255–76.

Cox, Harvey Gallagher. *The Future of Faith*. First ed. New York: HarperOne, 2009.

Giroux, Henry A. *The Violence of Organized Forgetting: Thinking Beyond America's Disimagination Machine*. San Francisco: City Lights, 2014.

Groome, Thomas H. *Will There Be Faith?* First ed. New York: HarperOne, 2011.

Hall, Douglas John. *When You Pray: Thinking Your Way into God's World*. Valley Forge: Judson, 1987.

Harris, Maria. *Fashion Me a People: Curriculum in the Church*. First ed. Louisville: Westminster John Knox, 1989.

Jenkins, Phillip. *The Next Christendom: The Coming of Global Christianity*. Third ed. New York: Oxford University Press, 2011.

55. Ibid., 150–58, 74.

56. Rodney, *How Europe Underdeveloped Africa*.

Jennings, Willie James. *The Christian Imagination: Theology and the Origins of Race*. Kindle ed. New Haven, Yale University Press, 2010.

Jeremias, Joachim. *The Prayers of Jesus*. Studies in Biblical Theology. Naperville, IL: A.R. Allenson, 1967.

Karimi, Faith. "Kenyan President Uhuru Kenyatta at ICC over Charges Linked to 2007 Violence." CNN, http://www.cnn.com/2014/10/08/world/africa/kenya-icc-status-hearing/.

Kelsey, David. *Imagining Redemption*. First ed. Louisville: Westminster John Knox, 2005.

Lee, Boyung. *Transforming Congregations through Community: Faith Formation from the Seminary to the Church*. First ed. Louisville: Westminster John Knox, 2013.

Little, Sara. *To Set One's Heart: Belief and Teaching in the Church*. Atlanta: John Knox, 1983.

Moore, Mary Elizabeth. *Teaching as a Sacramental Act*. Cleveland: Pilgrim, 2004.

Palmer, Parker J. *To Know as We Are Known: Education as a Spiritual Journey*. First ed. San Francisco: HarperSanFrancisco, 1993.

Procter-Smith, Marjorie. *Praying with Our Eyes Open: Engendering Feminist Liturgical Prayer*. Nashville: Abingdon, 1995.

Rodney, Walter. *How Europe Underdeveloped Africa*. Washington: Howard University Press, 1974.

Seymour, Jack L., ed. *Mapping Christian Education: Approaches to Congregational Learning*. Nashville: Abingdon, 1997.

———. *Teaching the Way of Jesus: Educating Christians for Faithful Living*. Nashville: Abingdon, 2014.

Seymour, Jack L., Margaret Ann Crain, and Joseph V. Crockett. *Educating Christians: The Intersection of Meaning, Learning, and Vocation*. Nashville: Abingdon, 1993.

Spelman, Elizabeth V. *Repair: The Impulse to Restore in a Fragile World*. Boston, Beacon, 2002.

Spong, John Shelby. *Honest Prayer*. Haworth, NJ: Christianity for the Third Millennium and St. Johann, 2000.

Wald, Priscilla. *Contagious: Cultures, Carriers, and the Outbreak Narrative*. Durham: Duke University Press, 2008.

7

A Pedagogy of Redemption
with Incarcerated Girls

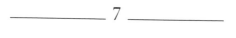

—————— *Evelyn L. Parker* ——————

PRISON RENDERS THE BODY of incarcerated girls as asexual or genderless. Because of identical clothes, prison cells, and recreational activities, they become indistinguishable from incarcerated boys. Such prison practices that ignore or intentionally deny God's gift of self-defined gendered bodies among incarcerated girls hinders the possibility of their holistic rehabilitation. What forms of pedagogy redeem and emancipate the bodies and minds of incarcerated girls? How are teachers redeemed in the teaching/learning process? This chapter explores the way pedagogy about women in the Bible helps incarcerated girls identify their bodies as worthy vessels of God. Thus, pedagogy with incarcerated girls is an act of redemption, for them and their teacher.

A redemptive community symbolizes daily living that ushers in justice and peace for all humankind, all creatures, and the earth. It offers salvation and freedom from death-dealing acts of racism, classism, sexism, ageism, heterosexism, and all other sins that physically destroy and psychologically debilitate God's good creation. A redemptive community, as empowered by the Holy Spirit, rescues, reclaims, and restores all of creation to God's gift of life that flourishes. The reach of a redemptive community extends to all peoples and contexts of the world that include girls in numerous contexts and circumstances such as incarcerated girls.

This chapter explores the way pedagogy about women in the Bible helps incarcerated girls identify their bodies as worthy vessels of God. I will explore two primary questions: What forms of pedagogy redeem and emancipate the bodies and minds of incarcerated girls? How are teachers redeemed in the teaching/learning process? Concretely, a pedagogy of redemption with incarcerated girls intends to give them skills for reading and interpreting scripture through an embodied pedagogical method; give incarcerated girls critical thinking/questioning skills; and facilitate wholesome body image among incarcerated girls – thus, viewing their bodies as "God Tangible Grace."

The context for teaching is the Dallas County Juvenile Detention Center in Dallas, Texas, where I taught girls ages 15-18 who are post adjudication and detained/incarcerated in the Residential Drug Treatment unit (RDT) for four to twelve weeks. Demographically the ten girls were 70 percent Latina, 20 percent African American and 10 percent European American from very poor and working poor households. The recidivism rate is high. It's not uncommon to see the same girl come back to the RDT Unit two to three times over a twenty-four month period. The Dallas County Juvenile Detention Center of which I speak is one of several complexes in the juvenile justice system of Dallas County, TX. The unit has a housing capacity of about 300 delinquent girls and boys as young as 10 years old. It is located on a hill overlooking Interstate 30 in the southwest sector of the city amid warehouses and other city government buildings. The detention center is also within a two- to five-mile-radius of several predominately African American and Latino neighborhoods. For a period of three years I taught Bible study with ten girls in the RDT on Sunday mornings for one hour at 10 a.m. The girls always elected to participate. There is never coercion or force.

I offer two case studies of teaching Bible study with adolescent girls in the Dallas County Juvenile Detention Center. The first case study recalls the events of teaching the passage from Luke 7:36–50, the nameless woman who anointed the feet of Jesus with her tears (the sinful woman forgiven). During this bible study session I read the scripture and asked the girls to listen particularly for the actions of the nameless woman. After reading the text I invited the girls to pretend they were the nameless woman, but to select a name they felt suitable for their characterization of her. After each girl named the woman I opened a bag of twelve scarves and invited the girls to choose one to adorn herself the way they thought their named woman (character) would wear the scarf. While the opportunity to give the woman in the text a name seemed intriguing, the invitation to adorn with scarves they would place in their personal property brought smiles, giggles, posing, and modeling. The girls wrapped their scarves in many creative and attractive ways. The gift of the scarves to adorn the woman in the Luke passage ignited vibrant conversation about the female character. When the Bible study ended one of the girls volunteered to pray as we held our hands over/under each other's without touching, holding confidence that the Holy Spirit connected our hands even though the detention center policy forbids touching/holding hands. The prayer was one of thanksgiving to God for fun while having "Church," the word the girls used for Bible study. I learned from that session that using scarves was a good decision that I would use again.

The second case study is a Bible study session with the same 10 incarcerated girls. This session involved the study of Exodus 15:20–21 where Miriam, the prophet, sings and dances after successfully crossing the Red Sea and escaping Pharaoh and his army. During this Bible study I invited someone to read the two verses after telling the story of the Israelites enslavement and flight to freedom. Again using the scarves, I invited the girls to create dances as if they were dancing with Miriam. While there was no music played, as they danced they swirled around and around. I asked how they felt dancing and the girls responded "happy" and some responded "silly." While there was not much reflection on what Miriam was doing and why it was clear they girls enjoyed creating dances with their scarves. The success of this session encouraged me to use liturgical dances for the interpretation of biblical texts of women in the Bible who also danced.

Redemptive Pedagogy for an understanding of the body as God's "tangible grace" with incarcerated teenage girls and their volunteer teacher.

The case studies above demonstrate my attempt to teach in a manner that invites incarcerated teenage girls who are 15-18 years of age to be restored in God's "tangible grace." It is within the juvenile detention center that girls are rendered asexual or gender neutral. Because of identical clothes and recreational activities incarcerated girls become indistinguishable from incarcerated boys. The gender neutral environment becomes more apparent when one observes how teenage girls and boys are moved about the detention center complex and how they eat and attend to bodily functions. Specifically, the detention center is not constructed to accommodate female incarcerated bodies, but male incarcerated bodies. The prison cell furniture (beds, chairs, toilets, showers, etc.) were designed for male bodies. The facilities do not accommodate mature female and occasionally pregnant female bodies.

Additionally, questions surface about the nature of rehabilitation in the RDT and other departments of the detention center. I raise these questions as a form of critique for rehabilitation in the United States juvenile justice system with girls in general. How is rehabilitation understood for incarcerated girls in general and specifically in a drug treatment unit? Is rehabilitation a set of structured activities to prepare a teenaged girl for re-entry into society? Does the preparation for re-entry consider sociocultural and socioeconomic issues unique to each girl? Does rehabilitation consider individual gender identity including how girls feel about themselves as female or non-female?

Yet, amid this gender neutral environment the girls are asked to embody or incarnate the concept of "tangible grace" along with their volunteer teacher. Tangible grace is a theological concept I developed to capture the notion that the human body is God's unconditional gift to ourselves and to others to be honored by the self and honored by other human beings.[1] The body is touchable grace to be honored regardless of color, ethnicity, gender, sexual identity, impediments, perfections, different/other abilities, diseased and non-diseased. Grace of this nature is non-saving in that the notions of unmerited favor or salvation of the human being is irrelevant. The grace of which I speak is an expression of God's goodness, blessings given to humanity in various forms.[2] The concept "tangible grace" signals the material expression of God's goodness that is the human body. This material concrete expression of God's goodness consists of billions of cells, organs, bone, sinew, connective tissue, limbs, and skin with systems for biological functioning. The human female body that menstruates, births, and lactates, or is incapable of these abilities, is a tangible expression of God's goodness to be protected, cared for, and adorned.

Specifically, the female adolescent body that is racially/ethnically African-American, Latina, European American, and mixed-race; that is pregnant, and recovering from drug addiction is "tangible grace." Most girls struggle with developing a healthy appreciation for their bodies. The problem of an unhealthy body image, however, is exacerbated when a girl is poor and also a racial/ethnic minoritized person. A healthy appreciation for a girl's body is complicated even more when she is incarcerated. Added

---

1. Parker, "Honoring the Body," 133–148.

2. McKim, *Westminster Dictionary of Theological Terms*, 120.

to being a poor Latina or a poor African American, incarcerated girls are often victims of crime. "According to the Department of Justice, 73 percent of girls behind bars have been sexually and physically abused; 40 percent have been raped. To escape abuse, many girls run away, skip school or act out."[3] "A study of delinquent girls in California found that 81 percent of chronically delinquent girls reported being physically abused; 56 percent reported sexual abuse. Another Study found that among detained girls, the median age of their first sexual encounter was [age] 7."[4]

Malika Saada Saar interviewed 100 incarcerated girls in New York, California, and Washington and discovered that more than half of the girls said they ran away from homes or foster care placements because they were being molested – only to be arrested for running away. The girls were angry they had been treated as criminals rather than victims of sexual assault. Other girls described running away from home and landing in the arms of sex traffickers.

The incarcerated girls in my class engage in recidivism because they find detention safer than being molested at home or being pimped on the street. The detention staff nicknamed repeat adolescent female offenders "frequent flyers." All these factors increase the likelihood of poor body image and low self-worth. Dominate culture as well as experiences of sexual abuse signal to poor racial/ethnic incarcerated girls that their bodies are undesirable and unworthy of protection and care.

In contrast, dominate cultural ideologies promote the thin, white/Euro, blue-eyed, blonde-haired body as the standard of beauty. Girls who fail to meet "the standard of beauty" are demonized for being "substandard." Sarah Grogan and Nicola Wainwright were among a few feminists during the late 1900s who examined body image and the influence of media among girls. Grogan and Wainwright argued " . . . that girls as young as 8 recognize and internalize dominant cultural pressures to be thin" in their 1996 essay titled "Growing up in a culture of slenderness: girls' experiences of body dissatisfaction."[5] "Their article is part of a wider psychological study of young women's body image and body (dis)satisfaction based on group interviews with white working and middle-class girls aged 8 and 13 from the UK."[6] They recommended that girls' bodies be more resilient against

3. Saar, "Girls Behind Bars," 102.

4. Ibid, 2.

5. Coleman, "The Becoming of Bodies," 165.

6. Ibid.

negative influences to healthy body image such as teenage magazines.[7] A study by Lisa Duke in 2000, titled "Black in a blonde world: race and girls' interpretations of the feminine ideal in teen magazines," examined whether girls read magazines critically and explored the role of race as an influencing factor for middle-class girls. While all the girls, ages 12-18, were middle-class, sixteen girls were African American, and ten were white girls. Whereas the white girls in Duke's study evaluated and defined themselves by their appearance, the African-American girls deemed personality and character more significant. Duke argues that the feminine ideal of beauty and slimness is less important to African-American girls partly because of the exclusion of images of black girls and women in magazines and partly because of African-American culture which has a

" . . . more realistic, inclusive view of the female physical norm . . . reinforced by elder female family members, who were said to view heavier girls as healthier, and by African-American men, who prize "thick or amply filled out girls as sexually appealing and desirable."[8]

While Lisa Duke's research may have validity for middle-class African-American girls, I question her findings regarding poor Black girls who are incarcerated. Anecdotal evidence of negative language such as being unattractive and self-mutilation suggests anything but viewing the Black female body as attractive.

A Redemptive Pedagogy with Incarcerated Girls

In the midst of such contextual issues, incarcerated girls are invited to love their bodies as God's touchable gift while experiencing selected texts about women in the Bible in a teaching/learning environment inside the detention center. How does an African-American, full-figured female with grey dreadlocks who comes to the detention center weekly teach the adolescent girls described above to understand themselves or claim identity as "God's tangible grace" in a sustained way regardless of being incarcerated or "in the free," the term incarcerated girls use to describe life outside the detention center? How do these two body types engage in teaching and learning that is emancipatory toward self-defined gendered bodies?

My search for a redemptive pedagogical method or process had four criteria:

7. Ibid.
8. Duke, "Black in a Blonde World," 385.

- The pedagogical method must facilitate embodiment of God's tangible grace.

- The method must include activities that engage the whole body of each girl, while honoring the detention center's policy of not touching each other.

- The method must engage the girls in practices of critical questioning (emancipatory learning) that are not practiced in a manner of the mind/body split.

- The method must be fun.

I appropriate some Augusto Boal's Theater of the Oppressed Laboratory (TOPLab) methods for teaching incarcerated adolescent girls. TOPLab methods fit the criteria for a pedagogical method. TOPLab is process of theatrical analysis and critiques that utilizes interaction between the audience and the performers. Ordinarily, the performers are nonprofessionals and may create scenarios/scenes for analysis, critique, and new potentially viable strategies for justice from their own experiences of injustice. Among the various theatrical forms are image, invisible, and forum theater. Boal's corpus also includes games and exercises that prepare "performers" for the theatrical forms. I have relied heavily on the games and exercises to teach biblical texts about women. I've used improvisation without a script, one line spoken by several actors, image of the word, image of the image, completing the image, and other image techniques. I have augmented image and improvisation techniques with props and costumes that "honor" the body of the character as interpreted by the actor/performer.

I have also invited the girls to dance the biblical text as they image the woman or girl in the text would dance. When dancing they can also adorn themselves with scarves they select that will be placed in their personal properties and taken with them upon release from the juvenile detention center. The full process involves:

- An introduction of the biblical text followed by a reading of the text by a volunteer or the teacher.

- Instructions are given that invites girls to create images, improve scenes, or dance the text

- Girls are invited to reflect on their "experience of the biblical text" sometimes in the moment as well as at the end of the activity while sitting around a table. Girls are asked to journal their questions, thoughts and feelings following activities.

A review of current literature on teaching incarcerated girls shows that theatre is the preferred pedagogical method. Authors that include Meade Palidofsky (2012), Maisaha Winn, and Chelsea Jackson (2011) have published articles on the use of theatre for rehabilitation of incarcerated adolescent girls. Palidofsky describes " . . . the evolution of an innovative program for incarcerated girls in which youth work collaboratively with theater professionals to create, develop, and perform musicals based on their experiences."[9] She examines the link between trauma (i.e. rape, neglect, abuse, etc.) and incarceration through the voices of the girls, as they appear in participants' writings and lyrics. The author offers anecdotal evidence of the therapeutic benefits of the theatrical program and implications for juvenile justice systems. The article by Jackson and Winn use a theatrical program with formerly incarcerated Black girls as a means of bridging from incarceration back to "their liberated lives" in their schools, communities, and families.[10]

Challenges

- Depending on the content of the biblical text, ordinarily most girls enjoy the process and express gratitude for encouraging them to think differently about scripture. Most importantly, girls express thanks for being encouraged to ask questions about the biblical text, which is a new experience for them. On the other hand, some girls find it strange and difficult to improvise or dance to their ideas/interpretations of scripture.

- Some girls have poor reading skills and are embarrassed to read aloud or express their interpretations of the biblical text. Care must be given to invite girls to read or express themselves in a way that does not embarrass them. Since girls can elect not to participate in the bible study, a lack of sensitivity can decrease the size of the group from ten to none.

---

9. Palidofsky, "Dramatic Healing," 239–256.

10. Winn and Jackson, "Toward a performance of possibilities," 615–620.

- Since a number of volunteer groups from churches and nonprofit religious groups visit with the girls each day of the week they bring various religious perspectives, which are primarily conservative evangelical. Interpreting the Bible using feminist/womanist hermeneutics of embodiment and through embodied methods is, to my knowledge, not offered by any other religious volunteer groups. Thus, this minority interpretative perspective must constantly compete with other perspectives.

Possibilities

- A theater pedagogical model holds the most promise for teaching/learning with incarcerated girls and their volunteer teacher.

- Palidofsky's model, as well as Jackson and Winn's theatrical models offer insights on how I might improve and expand my method. I can partner with theater professionals, such as the Theater Department at Meadows School of the Arts at Southern Methodist University, to develop a better emancipatory pedagogical model for embodying the concept of "God's Tangible Grace."

- An improved theater pedagogical model has the capacity to prepare adolescent girls to make positive life choices, heal from trauma, learn critical emancipatory methods of questioning, thus, becoming self-defined gendered persons who understand their bodies as God's gift to be honored.

Redemption of Our Bodies

In light of the teaching challenges and possibilities listed above, what is the vision for a redemptive community, empowered by the Holy Spirit which reclaims and restores incarcerated girls back to their schools, families, and friends where they can flourish? To answer this question we must clarify "redemptive community." This term is a group of people, such as a congregation or support group, that understand and are accountable for sustained deliverance of the incarcerated girl from death into life. A redemptive community incubates wholesome living for its constituents, even when faced with systemic injustices. In optimal conditions an incarcerated girl who views her body as God's touchable gift to be honored will be faced with insurmountable problems when she returns to a community that does not value her body or any female's body as God's gift to be honored. The struggle to maintain such a "transformed" mind will be extremely difficult. The redemptive community that will save incarcerated girls must arise from a redemptive pedagogy within the community itself. The vision for a redemptive community must be its own transformation into a salvific body through the power of the Holy Spirit working through teaching and learning that helps women and men honor their own bodies as God's grace. Once adults understand their bodies in this manner then they can act as redeeming communities. To be clear, I am not suggesting that a redeeming community is exclusively external to an incarcerated girl's community of origin (rural, inner-city). A redeeming community must be, first and foremost, the community of origin the community of origin — such as a congregation, support group, or peers—and simultaneously the external community, such as the city government.

The community of origin must experience a transformation of ideology where all human bodies are valued, particularly honoring female bodies. Just as communities saturated with crack and cocaine houses are transformed when local leaders surface to make members of the community aware of the death-dealing conditions in the community, so too must leaders rise up and raise awareness against violence against women and girls. When leaders learn to honor their bodies then they can honor the body of all women or girls. Such a community is redemptive. It creates its own power by transforming beliefs and practices about the bodies of women and men, boys and girls, and works to preserve and protect human life from within the community. While the community's power is spiritual and social, such communal power is the starting point for creativity that generates material power.

External communities that have socioeconomic and sociopolitical power become redemptive when they are transformed into communities that act for justice on behalf of communities that do not have material power. Middle and upper class communities have potential of becoming redemptive when they channel their material resources to address the systemic causes related to incarceration of girls. Systems that create poverty, inadequate education, and poor or substandard housing can be dismantled by communities that realize marginalized persons bodies are encumbered and dishonored through policies that render people to poverty. Redemptive communities dismantle such policies to create a just society.

The Church as Redemptive Community

While the material community of an incarcerated girl, her community of origin, and external material communities can be redemptive, the central redemptive community for incarcerated girls is the church, specifically the Christian ecclesial community and the local congregation. Following the command of Jesus Christ to go and make disciples of all peoples in Matthew 28:18–20, we know the mandate of his Church and its mission. It was to be a community of witness, proclaiming the kingdom which Jesus had first proclaimed, inviting human beings from all nations to saving faith. It was to be a community of worship, initiating new members by baptism in the name of the Holy Trinity. It was to be a community of discipleship in which the apostles, by proclaiming the word, baptizing, and celebrating the Lord's Supper, were to guide new believers to observe all that Jesus himself had commanded.[11]

Within this understanding of the Christian church, Jesus' proclamation of the kingdom offers clues to its redemptive nature. The operative phrases are discipleship and observance of all that Jesus commanded. These phrases are captured in the love and justice that Jesus Christ requires in the world today.

How does the Christian church or congregation extend love and justice to girls so they may thrive? First, love and justice become incarnate in a congregation that advocates for policies that support girls to prevent incarceration and rehabilitate them when they are released from prison. Girls prone to delinquent behavior need Christian women in their lives who are honest, worthy of respect, model good decision making, and are consistently available to them. Women with these characteristics are the "mothers" of congregations that participate in women's church auxiliaries. Those "mothers" of the congregation often are in the best position to mentor girls. Thus, congregational policy that advocates for girls mandates that relevant church auxiliaries include girls in their membership. The argument that roots this premise is women mentor girls best in natural environments such as the Women's Missionary Society of the Christian Methodist Episcopal Church, the United Methodist Women, and the Church Women United.

11. *The Church Towards a Common Vision*, Faith and Order Paper No. 214.

Such denominational and ecumenical women's organizations should be required by their congregations to include girls within the main body of the organization rather than as an appendage group.

Second, a congregation extends love and justice when its policies include education and advocacy regarding violence against women and girls. Statistics consistently indicate that high rates of women and girls are victims of domestic violence each day. Congregations need policies that require continuous formal teaching/learning settings regarding domestic violence. Imagine the impact an annual teach-in about domestic violence could have if mandated by the policy making branch of a denomination for all local congregations. Such denominational policy would hold member congregations responsible in a systematic way for domestic violence awareness. Local congregations would be reminded through this type of education that God requires that they act justly. This leads to the third response to the question above.

Love and justice become embodied when a congregation or denomination advocates for just public policy on behalf of women and girls. Congregations and denominations are called to advocate for women and girls by lobbying for local, state, and federal policies that promote their welfare. Policies that promote the well-being of women and girls include the Violence Against Women Act and Equal Rights Amendment, as well as Roe v. Wade and related policies on abortion. Congregations and denominations are called, as a matter of the justice God requires of them, to lobby for policies that give women and girls an opportunity to flourish.

Finally, in response to the question about how churches extend love and justice to enable girls to thrive, it is critical that congregations and denominations form partnerships with organizations involved in advocacy for women and girls. Those partnerships extend to financial support of and volunteer service or ministry with the partner organizations. Imagine a congregation that tithes to groups like Girls Inc., the Girls Scouts, and the American Association of University Women, and the Black Women's Roundtable. Consider the impact a congregation could have if represented on advisory or governing boards of partner organizations that advocate on behalf of women and girls. The depth of the impact—on the congregation, partner organization, and the women and girls for whom they advocate— multiplies when financial support is coupled with hands-on assistance and advocacy.

These four responses challenge congregations and denominations to take positive action to become redemptive communities as disciples of Jesus Christ by loving and seeking justice for girls to thrive.

Bibliography

Coleman, Rebecca. "The Becoming of Bodies: Girls, media effects, and body image." In *Feminist Media Studies* 8:2 (2008).

The Church Towards a Common Vision, Faith and Order Paper No. 214. Geneva, Switzerland: World Council of Churches Publication, 2013.

Duke, Lisa. "Black in a Blonde World: race and girls' interpretations of the feminine ideal in teen magazines." *Journalism & Mass Communications Quarterly* 77: 2 (2000) 367–392.

McKim, Donald K. *Westminster Dictionary of Theological Terms*. Louisville: Westminster John Knox, 1996.

Palidofsky, Meade. "Dramatic Healing: The Evolution of a Trauma-Informed Musical Theatre Program for Incarcerated Girls." *Journal of Child & Adolescent Trauma* 5:3 (July 2012) 239–256.

Parker, Evelyn L. "Honoring the Body" in *On Our Way*. Dorothy Bass and Susan Briehl, eds. Nashville: Upper Room, 2010.

Saar, Malika Saada. "Girls Behind Bars" *Essence* 44:5 (September 2013).

Winn, Maisha T. and Chelsea A. Jackson. "Toward a performance of possibilities: resisting gendered (in)justice" in *International Journal of Qualitative Studies in Education* 24:5 (Sept/Oct 2011) 615–620.

8

Identity and Leadership Formation in Process in African American Adolescent Boys

—— *Carmichael Crutchfield* ——

IT WAS IN 1992, while I was working with African American adolescent boys in a rite of passage program I developed, that I first discovered my passion for identity development in African American boys and young men. Enlightened Males emerged through a fellowship from the Congress of National Black Churches based in Washington, D.C., which provided me the opportunity to be involved 24 hours a week for a year working with African American boys in Covington, Tennessee. It was a wonderful opportunity to combine and integrate three experiences I had during that year: working as a local pastor in the city of Covington, working for the social service agency, and advancing at seminary toward a Master of Divinity degree.

After finishing seminary in 1993, I continued involvement with the Enlightened Males program as a ministry, as academic research, and as a community project. Although the EM program is ongoing and I remain connected to it as a denominational executive, it was during 2006 that I was last totally immersed in the program.

Developing Enlightened Males

Enlightened Males grew out of my deep care and concern for African American adolescent males at this critical juncture in their lives. Having journeyed that way myself some years ago, I feel compassion for this poignant moment in the developmental process of our black sons. My research in this area brings me to the conviction that, beginning in adolescence, identity is formed through increasingly taking agency for one's own choices. For African American boys, gender and culture are two key aspects of identity formation during adolescence.

Enlightened Males is a year-long program which involves meeting with a group of eight boys twice a month for three hours, going on field trips together, meeting and talking with their parents (mothers mainly), and visiting some of their churches. I had known most of the boys longer than the one year of the program, two as their former pastor and three others through attendance at their church. The program culminates with a rites of passage program which took place that year during the last week in December 2006. This program's success depended on the volunteerism of church members and, in this case, a group of men who belong to a graduate chapter of the African American fraternity of which I am a member.

Convinced of the importance of positive African American adult male role models to aid in their journeys, the EM program was designed to surround the boys with such men—from pillar organizations in the African American context like congregations, the community, and African American fraternities. Since formation involves continual shaping and traditioning in a way of being and doing, rites of passage and ritual were woven into the EM program from its inception. Peer mentoring and leadership was another important aspect of the program and boys who completed the rite of passage were invited to join the group of adult men in leading the program the next year (with the added benefit of continuing those beneficial mentoring relationships).

While it is difficult to measure the success of a program like EM, I have found that the stories of the growth and development of the boys involved provide a point of reference for assessing the value of this program. To that end, let me share the stories of four of the boys who were part of the EM program for a season. I chose these four because their age places them in the adolescent stage of life, a particularly crucial point of development.

A Glimpse of Tom's Story

One of the boys that I will call Tom[1] was a 17 year old junior who was on the tennis team of his high school. Tom is the one I called "Mr. Cool" be-

1. Names throughout this chapter have been replaced by pseudonyms. In some

cause he was laid back and never seemed to get upset about things, as if he wanted others to think he didn't care. His attitude was akin to those young men who grown-ups are continually admonishing to pull up their pants. Tom often wore sun glasses, even indoors. He lived alone with his mother in the newest subsidized housing offered in the city. His mother had no job and spent a great deal of time with her son, keeping up with his activities. His grandmother also lived in the city and was involved in his life. I never heard him mention his father or a father figure. He had other siblings who lived in other places.

Tom attended church regularly with his mother, although he didn't say much about his actual involvement. He had opportunities outside of the home to be involved in social activities and took advantage of them as often as he could. Tom had a job and friends who helped him get around, since he didn't have access to a car. At the time I was not sure if his mother owned a car; I only saw her drive a car once. His mother was always concerned about him making the meetings. I remember her saying words to the effect of, "Rev. Crutchfield, can you pick him up?" once prior to a meeting. I actually picked him up for several meetings and someone always dropped him off. This was significant because we discouraged being a shuttle service for the EM boys to ensure the boys and their families took responsibility for some portion of their involvement.

When we first started our work together with an activity focused on problem solving, Tom would be inattentive. He would sometimes fall asleep or play with his phone. Occasionally, someone would get his attention. It was only after several sessions that he began to pay attention. I was convinced the difference came about as Tom began to respond to the additional attention given him by some of the adult men involved in the program. We saw in Tom a young man who had fallen into the all-too-common trap of believing education was not very important. At a point during our year together, it seemed that, with the help of the other men, he was becoming more engaged in the program's learning activities. Although it seemed simple, paying attention was difficult for Tom.

I found Tom to be an average student who had lost focus on education. He participated in program activities but with very little contribution to the discussions. He struggled as a reader. Interestingly, on our field trips, Tom was very sociable but would have the tendency to retreat into using his

---

cases, identifying information may have been modified to protect the boys and their families.

cell phone or listening to music. He had "street sense"—he knew what was happening on the streets. When I would ask about the events of the week in the city, Tom would always know some story of deviant behavior. He would talk to the other boys in the program as though he was their senior; in truth, he was. He referred to his juniors as "little buddy." He indicated that nickname meant they were very young. He seemed to enjoy giving all of those "little buddies" a hard time.

Tom was very respectful to adults. For example, I remember one field trip while I was driving, he made a point of telling me that the song on the radio was not the version he listened to. He brought this up apologetically because we had just discussed that particular artist and the derogatory music he produced. I could sense that he didn't want to offend or disappoint me.

From the very first encounter with Tom I noticed several things about him. He dressed nicely for the style he chose. He did not talk much. He always seemed to be on the phone. He knew every song and artist. He knew something about African American fraternities like the one in which some of our adult male volunteers held membership. His mom was invested in him and wanted him in the program to the point of making transportation arrangements for him. Tom was always talking about cars and was interested in the cars I drove. I think he thought I owned a lot of cars, a conclusion he drew unaware that these were often rental cars.

We went on one overnight trip to Little Rock, Arkansas, mainly to see the Clinton Presidential Library. Tom was energized and talked to the younger boys like he really was an experienced traveler. He was not totally engaged while at the library, but meals were an absolute joy for him. He got into an interesting interchange with one of the servers at a restaurant. It seemed he was trying to show his "street smarts," however, the server was older and smarter. Tom was at ease eating out, which was not the case with all the boys.

We took the boys, including Tom, to a leadership conference over 200 miles from home that lasted three days. When I came back to pick them up at the end of the conference, I was not surprised by Tom's complaints about the food and room—neither seemed acceptable to me either. However, I was shocked to hear him complaining about the behavior and attitudes of the boys who came from different states. I am not sure why it surprised me—maybe I underestimated his development and formation. He had never mentioned previously the unacceptable behavior of his peers, and there were occasions where it would have been appropriate. Perhaps the ones he was complaining about were strangers and whom he knew he would not see again. He was very descriptive about what he observed in their behavior, a conversation which allowed us to talk about what it meant to be a leader which was one of the EM program goals.

I was really impressed by the note Tom wrote concerning his experience at the conference. It seemed he had learned much about leadership while attending the conference. I looked forward to him coming to inspire the new group of boys as young men who went through the rite of passage were invited back the next year to take some leadership role in the program. Unfortunately, I was unable to be actively involved in the program the following year and lost track of Tom.

Jim's Story

Jim was a 16-year-old junior and a band member at his high school. He lived with his mother, father, and his 8 or 9 year old sister. His older brother, 24, recently finished college and was living at home again. His mother and father were professional educators and lived in a moderately nice house in an older neighborhood. Jim attended church and school activities and was in the process of learning to drive. He was not really interested in doing anything beyond what was necessary, so he was only involved in church and school because it was his parent's will. His parents were actively involved in his life.

Jim was the quietest one of the group of boys in the rite of passage program. I had known him for a long time, having been his pastor and so was particularly interested in Jim's identity formation. My deeper interest in Jim also was directly related to my wife and I having a strong friendship with his parents. We would sometimes babysit Jim, and his quietness was almost frightening. He would become so absorbed in watching television that sometimes he forgot to eat. At 16, Jim still behaved like a little boy in many ways. He only spoke when asked a direct question and then only very briefly. It seemed Jim did listen very well. When asked questions about what he had seen on TV or a video, he was quick to respond. I observed that Jim was very visual. He had been playing handheld computer games for most of his life, and he loved watching cartoons on TV. He was, however, not very verbal. People like Jim who seem quiet or less verbal have long intrigued me, particularly the evolution of their leadership qualities.

Another thing that stood out about Jim was his focus, particularly regarding his vocational goals. A typical group exercise in the program was to discuss the oft-asked question: What do you want to be when you grow up (occupation)? Jim always answered "to be a chief chef." Our group's pattern was then to follow up with the question: What do you have to do to reach your goal? Jim had already done some research and knew what it took to become a chief chef. He attended a new high school that offered a variety of classes geared toward technology and vocational education. Jim took courses where he learned about being in the restaurant and dining business.

Jim's self-esteem was boosted because he was in the band and earned leadership roles due to his excellent accomplishments with his horn. He was an above average student who had tremendous support from his two parents who both had master's degrees in education.

On our field trips, Jim would either play his games with his hand held device or sleep on the bus. He walked nonchalantly so it was difficult to know if he was enjoying what he was seeing or just going through motions. One of the places we toured was the National Civil Rights Museum in Memphis. Jim walked slowly through the site, occasionally reading, but mostly alone. He traveled at his own pace. It was difficult to have a real conversation with Jim, but he would answer questions. I knew that he was gaining from the experience because he was able to coherently answer questions—he might even say more than two or three words. When we went to an NBA game to see the Memphis Grizzlies play, Jim did not appear to be interested in the game. Although he was the only boy in the group who had experienced a professional basketball game before, he spent more time playing his handheld games than watching the game. He was not excited about going overnight on trips or going anywhere, period. These were not new experiences for him. He was the only boy who I never heard ask a question throughout our year together in the program. However, Jim always knew answers to questions related to videos or movies; this was further evidence to me that he was truly a visual learner. After graduation Jim did go to school and became a chef. He has not yet reached his goal of chief chef, but all indications are that he will reach it.

The Story of Roy

Another boy in the EM program, Roy, was a 13-year-old eighth grader who played football at his middle school. Roy was the youngest in the group.

He was an interesting and interested young man. He asked many questions and was very outgoing. Roy spoke often about how the men in the program had helped him and how he loved being in their presence. Roy would arrive early at the meetings and offered his help in arranging the room. He was familiar with the space because the meetings were held at his local church. He would talk to all of us adults prior to the meeting and tell us how much he liked coming to EM. He was glad to be with the older boys and didn't mind when he was teased with names like "little buddy." Roy was not small in stature, but his youthfulness was evident in that he wanted to play more than the older boys did.

Roy was always the first one to respond to questions. He was good at understanding the lessons in Black history which we taught in a variety of ways. When asked about his goals, he would always respond that he wanted to be a football player. He talked about going to the University of Tennessee in Knoxville and then being drafted to play football professionally—a pretty unrealistic goal for even the most talented among us. Over the course of our time together, Roy began saying he wanted to be a football player *and* a lawyer. I even heard him respond once, "If I don't make it as a football player, I can be a lawyer." He just had begun playing football in middle school.

To my surprise, Roy was getting only average grades in school. We talked about the subjects giving him trouble, and I encouraged him to seek help. Looking back, I can see one of the weaknesses of the EM program was that we didn't do enough one-on-one mentoring like this.

At one of the last meetings, while discussing education and choices, we had a discussion of the consequences to the choices we make. Roy spoke about his oldest brother who was 19 at the time, how talented he was at track and field until he dropped out of school. Roy talked about his brother's choices of alcohol and cigarettes which impacted his body to the point where he was no longer able to run at all. He would say, "My brother is lost, but he keeps telling me not to get involved in drugs." In contrast to Tom and Jim, Roy and his brother David (who I will describe next) didn't dress with the latest fashions or own cell phones or iPods. However, they lived in a nice house in a new subdivision with their mom. Their mom, who was not very available, was the one parent who failed to respond personally to any of my correspondence.

Roy seemed connected to his spirituality and was always quick to pray when a volunteer was asked to do so prior to eating at the meetings. He was very articulate and his prayers had depth and thought for a 13-year-old. Roy loved to eat and was always interested in knowing what we were going to eat; he was always the winner in the amount consumed!

On our field trips, Roy would be the "life of the party." He had a wonderful sense of humor and laughed often. He chattered on about what was happening in his school, focusing with the greatest energy on the inconsistencies he saw in school discipline. Sometimes after listening to him, even I found myself wanting to get up and go to school and address his concerns. This was an area where one-on-one contact was needed to help the boys learn how to productively address injustice and hypocrisy. Roy played football in high school, but not in college. He is still trying to find his way but is positive about life.

David's Story

Roy's brother was also involved in the EM program; I will call him David. He was a 16-year-old junior and played baseball at his high school. As I mentioned when describing Roy, he and David lived with their mother in a very nice subdivision outside of the city limits. Their mother worked long hours and spent very little time with them. Their father was absent from their lives—even the mention of father caused David to become very upset. David loved his little brother Roy and was always encouraging him and speaking kind words about him. David was quick to talk about God—more so than any other boy in the group. I describe David as very serious, compassionate, and emotionally expressive.

Both David and his younger brother, Roy attended and were actively involved in church activities thanks to a strong church youth leader. Outside of church and school activities they had few opportunities outside of their home. They neither drove nor had access to a car. Their mom did not attend church.

David was one of only a few African Americans on his high school baseball team. He apparently was like his oldest brother, the former track star, in that he was also very fast; he told me they would put him in when he was younger to pinch run for others. David talked much about the experience of playing baseball. It was evident he took a deep sense of pride in being on the team. He was also on the football team but didn't play much.

David was very thoughtful and responsive. He tried hard to say and do what he thought would please the adults. For example, for the leadership conference that I mentioned earlier, David was late with his paperwork. When I asked him about it, he made an excuse about having a hard time getting in touch with a guidance counselor to verify his information. For one thing, he said, she was only available at a certain time of the day and David had to wait for someone to be available to drive him. The story seemed improbable. Later, I learned David's grade point average was below the qualifying GPA for the leadership conference. I was convinced that David had such a strong desire to attend that he didn't want to disappoint me by admitting his grades were too low. I regret we did not take the opportunity to further discuss or explore with him why he did not disclose the truth about his grades.

Fortunately, grace reigned and David was permitted to attend the conference after all. It was a wonderful opportunity for him since he had never been out of the state of Tennessee. Personally, I was pulling for him. He had never actually been on a college campus and before coming to our program he really had low aspirations for his abilities. When asked the question, "What do you want to be?" David replied consistently, "a truck mechanic." When asked, as was our pattern, "How do you get there?" it was clear he had researched and knew the path. I admit, however, that I was not sure he was always in touch with reality. For instance, when we would talk about grades he spoke about working to raise his GPA in ways that were mathematically impossible. I realize now that David simply might not have understood the math involved in calculating GPA.

There's one final observation about David that bears sharing. I was visiting his church one Sunday (before he had become a part of the program), and after worship I discovered him in the choir area crying. Later, trying to understand what I encountered, his pastor and I discussed this. She told me she had gone one Sunday evening to David's home to visit, and it seemed to her that David felt overwhelming pressure to take care of the house and his younger brother Roy while his mother worked. Along with that, David and Roy's older brother was estranged from the family, and David missed the brother being around and helping out with things at home. David even expressed anger toward his overworked mother and absent father. What the pastor described seemed to me like David might have been experiencing role confusion typical of adolescence. David was a wreck from the stress and, as sometimes happens in the Black church, something in worship touched him deeply and triggered the outburst of tears that Sunday.

The pastor was a great help to David. His youth director was like a second mother to him; her son became like a brother to David. During one of our times of sharing while David was in the program, he spoke of these people who were now in his life and the impact they made. David also spoke highly of the effects the EM program had on him and his brother. At the same time he spoke appreciatively of his mother and her providing for them. One day while I was driving him home, David told me about how hard his mother worked to provide for them; on other occasions he had shared about how his mom was always gone. David finished high school and went on for training as an auto mechanic. I lost track of him and do not know if he fulfilled his dream.

Rite of Passage and Mentoring as a Bridge for Adolescent Boys

All four of these boys had parental guidance in various forms. They knew something about respect for others and conducted themselves in ways generally acceptable in African American church culture (mainly giving respect to adults). All four are, in my estimation, at the conventional level of reasoning on Lawrence Kohlberg's scale. They had a basic understanding of conventional morality and reason and tended to be self-identified with rules, upholding them consistently. Within this level, I believe they were at Kohlberg's stage 3: aware of shared feelings, agreements, and expectations, which take primacy over individual interests. According to Kohlberg, persons at stage 3 define what is right in terms of what is expected by people close to oneself, and in terms of the stereotypic roles that define being good, e.g., a good brother, mother, teacher. Therefore being good means keeping up mutual relationships using tools such as trust, loyalty, respect, and gratitude. Their perspective is that of the local community or family; there is not as yet within them a consideration of the generalized social system.[2] I realize an argument could also be made for all four of the boys being in stage 4 of the conventional level of reasoning where a shift takes place from defining what is right in terms of local norms and role expectations to defining right in terms of the laws and norms established by the larger social system. This is the "member of society" perspective in which one is moral by fulfilling the actual duties defining one's social responsibilities; for example, one must obey the law except in extreme cases in which the law comes into conflict

2. Kohlberg and Turiel, *Moral Development and Moral Education*, 20.

with other prescribed social duties. Obeying the law is seen as necessary in order to maintain the system of laws, which protect everyone.[3] It is this example that causes me to be hesitant in moving any of the four boys completely into stage 4. I am convinced these four boys obey laws only out of a sense of staying out of trouble with the law and their parents.

Using the framework of James Fowler's faith development theories, I find it challenging to try to assess where Tom, Jim, Roy, and David fit. Based not only on my encounters with these boys during our meeting times, but also through other opportunities to observe and have further conversations with Roy, David, and Jim,[4] my best hunch is that they were in stage 2 mythic-literal faith, at least by the time we finished our year together. This is the stage in which the person begins to take on for himself or herself the stories, beliefs, and observances that symbolize belonging to his or her community. Beliefs are appropriated with literal interpretations, as are moral rules and attitudes, and symbols are taken as one-dimensional and literal. Story becomes the major way those at this stage begin to connect with the themes and ideas of the faith. Those in this stage are drawn into and connect powerfully with the cosmic stories of the faith with their anthropomorphic characters and detailed narratives. They do not, however, have the capacity yet to step back from the detail and flow of the stories to reflect on the larger conceptual meanings. In the mythic-literal stage, the meaning is conveyed by and "trapped" in the narrative.[5] Jim, David and Roy definitely had adopted the beliefs of their church communities. Each had been through classes and experiences in the church that helped form them in the Christian community. Additionally, for David and Roy they had been formed in identity as part of our EM program and wanted to continue in the process. I attribute this largely to the men leading the program.

The EM program was developed specifically for adolescent African American males to provide impactful experiences and relationships for them at a very crucial stage of their lives. It was the work of Erik Erikson that informed the rationale and curriculum for this program. Adolescents are deeply engaged in establishing their own identity. At the same time, internal and external pressures such as the need to be accepted can lead to confusion and overdependence on peer approval. Couple this psychosocial

---

3. Ibid.

4. I cannot comment on Tom's faith development because I didn't have the same depth and frequency of experience with him that I had with the other three boys.

5. Conn, *Women's Spirituality*, 226–232.

confusion with being a black child who has a statistically significant probability of living in poverty—and developing a positive identity becomes very difficult. The EM program was created to inspire and foster leaders for the future. The program's goal was, and continues to be, helping boys develop a positive self-image which will propel them to live into their God-given vocation with excellence. It is from this spirit that leaders are made.

Issues of identity were the catalyst in creating a prayer to be used at the beginning of each EM meeting. It is my contention that, from adolescence onward in life, development of one's identity comes about as a result of what one *does* as opposed to what *is done to them.* The prayer was created to foster this sense of agency in participants. At each meeting the same prepared prayer was used to help form the boys' identity in a way that grappled and struggled with identity, social interactions, and moral issues.

With identify formation as one of the major concerns of the EM program, Erikson's theories provided foundation. Erikson understood the process of identity formation to be lifelong, and he was particularly interested in charting progressive strength in ego identity—often in response to increasingly complex life challenges—which he described using stages. For Erikson, each person possessed at least three distinct identities: ego identity or "the self," personal identity or the qualities and characteristics that make each person unique, and social identity or the social and cultural roles each person plays. Under development in any of these areas can increase the chance of a crisis of identity or role confusion.[6] Two primary areas of identity were addressed and strengthened in the EM program: gender and culture.

I have an overarching concern regarding leadership formation in African American males, and I argue that this involves, first and foremost, identity formation. Thus, when developing programs for leadership formation in African American males, I begin with identity formation. As mentioned earlier, I believe identification largely to be related to culture and gender. However, I contend that identity formation must be considered from a psychoanalytic perspective, as well, in order to aid in leadership formation of individuals. Both are part of understanding adolescents in general and black male adolescents specifically. Identity builds on meaning made by the individual from their pre-adult experiences which prepare adolescents for the tasks of adulthood. Identity is essentially a synthesis of unique personal capacities, values, significant identifications (and fantasies) with plans, ideals, expectations and opportunities. A major source of

6. Cote and Levine, *Identity Formation, Agency and Culture,* 17.

strain and crisis during adolescence arises from the formation and integration of this combination of qualities, skills, values and interests.

The EM program was designed to directly impact the adolescent male during this crucial period in life when adolescents are facing so many simultaneous demands while, at the same time, are involved in competition of various forms in the midst of psychosocial self-definition.[7] Having moved beyond childhood, and not yet fully adults, adolescents find themselves in a transitional period between statuses and affiliations, characterized by rootlessness and a high degree of change. It is during late adolescence, according to Erikson, that the individual tries to conceptualize the self, to access what one *has been* as a child, *is* now, and *would like to be* in the future.[8] Taylor points out that there is little evidence that black adolescents are any less affected by the stress and strain of the period than other youths. Indeed, there is evidence that minority group status and associated disadvantages amplify the stress and further complicate this transition for black adolescents.[9]

Recognizing this "double jeopardy"—typical adolescent development coupled with the added stresses African American males encounter—is helpful as we consider leadership formation in black males. Adolescence is a time when choice and commitment become dominant themes in the struggle for identity-formation. Indeed, the move toward commitment is so serious and so significant that providing healthy conditions to let it unfold becomes just as crucial for human development as providing healthy growth in early childhood.[10]

Therefore, leadership formation in adolescents is largely dependent upon society (in the broadest sense possible) providing conditions that foster development. That means our concern for the social, economic, and political welfare of youth is warranted not only from a physical and theological standpoint, but from a formational and a developmental viewpoint. I argue—and I believe the church supports me in this—that the community and family must partner in a holistic fashion, working in political, social, and economic arenas as well as attending to spiritual care. The formation and development of our youth is dependent upon our involvement,

7. Taylor, *Black Youth*, 156.

8. Ibid., 157.

9. Ibid.

10. Ibid.

influence and motivation—in short, it is dependent on our leadership as adults. This is what some call the "village approach" to ministry.

Erikson concurs when he writes that the development of a healthy identity "depends on a certain degree of choice, a certain hope for our individual chance, a conviction in freedom of self-determination."[11] The need to develop a sense of identity from among all past, current, and potential relations compels youth to make a series of increasingly more circumscribed selections of personal, vocational, and ideological commitments. These choices entail " . . . the emotional, intellectual and sometimes physical reach for other people as well as ideals, ideologies, causes, and work choices. The range of possibilities is not unlimited, however, and is likely to be greatly influenced by the institutional or socio-cultural contexts within which youths find themselves."[12]

One of the foundational aspects of the EM program is ritual, grounded in this concern for fostering healthy identity formation. One aspect of the program's ritual involves the prayer mentioned earlier. Although the intent of the program is not to teach Christianity, we spend time not only praying the prayer but discussing its meaning and choice of words. The program also has two standard poems that are part of its rituals. The first, entitled "I Am a Gentleman," is anonymously written and the other, "A Pledge To My Self," was authored by Mychal Winn. As part of the program's adaptable curriculum, participants join in the ritual of reading in unison eleven statements about what it means to be an enlightened male. Finally, we share in the ritual of eating together.

Rituals have been a longstanding part of African culture. They help give meaning to religion, but also to life. Throughout the EM program, from the commitment ceremony through the rite of passage at the end, ritual plays an important role in our activities. Erikson claims a cultural value for ritualization in:

1. elevating immediate personal needs into a broader communal context,

2. teaching good ways to do simple and practical tasks of everyday life,

3. deflecting feelings of unworthiness on others without and within the culture,

4. confirming identity and the stages that it must pass through,

11. Ibid., 158.

12. Ibid., 157.

5. lacing cognitive patterns of thought in service of a shared communal vision,

6. developing sacramental meaning in particular activities, and

7. developing a moral imagination, a kind of ethical discernment.[13]

It is in the context of the ritualization of everyday life that we construct a moral and human universe—the contexts we make, live, and break. Erikson provides yet another way of seeing the situations we are in (context) and the fragmentation of perspective (conditionality). Context/ritualization help us know our doing, grant our doing credence, and have it, in turn, sustain us. In doing—both that which is small and routine as well as that which is public and significant—we operate within a vision. "Visions are grounded in facts verifiable in some detail and yet arranged to fit within a cosmology and an ideology that unite groups of human beings in mutual actualizations."[14]

In practice, some of the boys were more responsive to some of the program's rituals than to others. For example, Roy and David were always very open to defining words in the prayer. While it is true that not all rituals impacted each of the boys in the same way, I contend that the rituals of prayer, pledges, meals, etc., did prompt reflection and questioning—one of the key visions of what we intended EM to be and do.

Roy, the 13-year-old, was particularly drawn to the words about handling anger in a productive way. He once sparked a lengthy discussion about this subject. William Pollack's book, *Real Boys*, is helpful in providing a lens through which we can understand Roy's issues. I see that Roy was dealing with some of the "boy codes"[15] at school. In reality, it is difficult for boys to walk away or not say anything when they feel they have been mistreated. I continue to find this one of the hardest things to teach boys who live in a world of violence. Each year it seems to be more challenging—and increasingly important. The EM curriculum devotes a session to dealing with anger which, along with mentoring from the men in leadership, seemed to make a difference.

13. Erikson, "Toys and Reason: Stages in Ritualization of Experience," http://www.wvu.edu/~lawfac/jelkins/mythweb99/ritual.html (accessed 03/15/2010).

14. Ibid.

15. William Pollack speaks of "Boy Codes" in his work *Real Boys* as he and co-author Mary Pipher refer to certain societal expectations of boys.

The development of cultural identity in these boys was of crucial importance in the program. To that end, we spent many sessions on Black History, viewing videos, reading articles, and searching the Internet for stories of our history. We encouraged the boys to reflect upon what they had seen and heard. It is not always easy to determine progress in formation, but from my observations of Tom, Jim, Roy, and David it seemed to me that each had grasped more of their culture over the 12 months of the program. They probably didn't know a great deal more facts, but I am convinced they were more knowledgeable of their history—"the root to their blossoming tree," to quote one of the pledges we used in the ritual of the program. We also spent time discussing what this phrase meant.

Conclusion.

Writing the Foreword of *The State of Black America in 2007*, then Senator Barack Obama, now president of the United States, wrote:

> "In some cities, more than half of all black boys do not finish high school, and, by the time they are in their thirties, almost six in ten black high school dropouts will have spent time in prison. Half of black men in their twenties are jobless, and one study a few years ago found more black men in prison than enrolled in college."[16]

I contended in 1992 and continue to say today that the only enduring solution is reaching our boys and showing them a better way. This is a very tedious and demanding task, and one that cannot wait.

The rationale of the Enlightened Males program goes beyond drug abuse and crime prevention. Of course these should result. However, we want far more for these boys. We hope to inspire and develop leaders for the future. The program's goal is to help adolescent African American males develop positive self-images which will propel them to be the very best they can be, their truest God-given selves. It is from that spirit that leaders are made. The EM program strives to this day to open doors for young men and help them see the hope and the future God has for them, to create redemptive community in the lives of these boys, their churches, and their communities.

---

16. *The State of Black America, Portrait of the Black Male*, 11.

Bibliography

Conn, Joann Wolski, ed. *Women's Spirituality: Resources for Christian Development*, Maltwah, NJ: Paulist, 1986.

Cote, James E. and Charles Levine. *Identity Formation, Agency and Culture*. Maltwah, NJ: Lawrence Erlbaum Associates, 2002

Crutchfield, Carmichael. *The Enlightened Males Program Manual*. Washington, DC: Congress of National Black Churches, Inc., 1993.

Erikson, Erik. "Toys and Reason: Stages in Ritualization of Experience." http://www.wvu.edu/~lawfac/jelkins/mythweb99/ritual.html

Harder, Arlene F. "The Developmental Stages of Erik Erikson" http://www.learningplaceonline.com/stages/organize/Erikson.htm

Kohlberg, Lawrence and Elliot Turiel, *Moral Development and Moral Education*. G. Lesser, ed. Chicago: Scott Foresman, 1971.

Pollack, William and Mary Pipher. *Real Boys: Rescuing Our Sons from the Myths of Boyhood*. New York: Owl, 1999.

The State of Black America, Portrait of the Black Male. National Urban League. New York: Beckman, 2007.

Taylor, Ronald. *Black Youth, Role Models and the Social Construction of Identity in Black Adolescents*. Reginald L. Jones, ed. Berkeley, CA: Cobb and Henry, 1989.

9

Redemptive Community Across Generations

Welcoming Youth and Young Adults

Denise Janssen

VITAL CONGREGATIONS NEED A healthy mix of people of all ages across generations in order to thrive. However, it is readily observable that this mix of generations complicates community life. Conflicts and different assumptions too often divide people, and these are sometimes exaggerated by generational differences. How are youth treated? How are new members welcomed? Are older persons ignored or might they be revered in ways that fail to take them seriously as unique individuals? When there is mutuality and when the complications of being church together across generations are engaged with intentionality, those same vital congregations can become spaces of redemption and hope for people across generations.[1]

One need not investigate very deeply or have much more than a casual relationship with the church to recognize that *redemptive* is frequently not a word that would come to mind when describing relationships (or the lack of them) across generations in the typical local congregation. At its best, the congregation provides a supportive and hospitable place for people to love God and neighbor, to discern vocation, to learn and grow in faith, to do more together than each could individually—ultimately, to make meaning of the day-to-day of life. Congregations and the people who comprise them are works-in-progress and make mistakes as they practice their faith and seek to

---

1. The material in this chapter first appeared in my book, *Reclaimed: Faith in an Emerging Generation.* Valley Forge: Judson, 2015. It has been revised substantially for this chapter. © Judson 2015. Used by permission.

become more whole. Allow me to illustrate with couple of examples, one told by a young adult and the other from the perspective of an older adult:

- Bethany was stunned. Back in worship at the "Christmas-and-Easter-and-when-my-parents-visit" church of her twenties, she found herself dumbstruck at the way she had just been treated. She had been engaged in worship on this Sunday when she attended on her own, sensing that she just needed some peace and the church had at least been good for that. The pastor, a fortysomething woman, invited the congregation to join her in reading the scripture text for the day. Bethany found the text intriguing and wanted to read it again for herself, perhaps in another translation. She had just called up the scripture on her phone to have another look when the woman in front of her turned around and chastised her loudly enough for everyone around to hear. "That's just disrespectful!" the woman, whom Bethany didn't know, admonished, assuming Bethany was "just messing around" on her phone rather than paying attention.

- Marion retired to an area near her children and found herself, at nearly eighty, searching for a new congregation. At coffee with a friend, she bemoaned the way congregations she visited seemed to assume, because she moved more slowly and had gray hair, that she held conservative values and resisted change. The congregations she visited routed her toward the "older adult ladies" Sunday school class and the seniors' lunch group. But Marion loved change and new experiences, and she loved to be around younger people. Their ideas were invigorating to her and their energy was contagious. In young people, she intimated, she found joy and hope. Marion died several years later before she found a congregation where she found connections to life-affirming younger people among whom she sought to learn and be inspired.

In reality, congregations and the people in them continually fail to live up to the ideals they espouse. This is part of being human, created in the image of God, works-in-progress, on the journey. This reality, however, can be particularly problematic for those who have not yet come to grips with their own inconsistencies and hypocrisies. While that could describe anyone across the life cycle, it frequently characterizes adolescents and young adults who tend to have highly tuned sensitivities to incongruence and injustice, who are beginning to claim their own adult voice and sense of agency. Since affiliating with a congregation is increasingly optional—even counter-cultural in the U.S.—there are few external forces pushing us to reach across generational divides and reconcile these issues. The ripple effects of these rifts and fissures go far beyond the church, but let's focus there for now.

Being Church Together: The Grace of Resilience and Enough of the Right Stuff

In research I conducted over the last few years, I interviewed young adults active in congregations who, when they were adolescents, were also actively engaged in congregations.[2] From those interviews emerged several areas of convergence in what I heard from them. The young adults I interviewed, now actively engaged in ministry through a congregation, described ways in which their active involvement in the congregations of their youth succeeded and fell short in four key areas:

1. fostering healthy identity entanglements with their faith,

2. making space for them to use their still emerging voices and discern vocation,

3. nurturing them with the sacrament of genuine relationships, and

4. tethering them during times of faithful fallowness.[3]

These four areas seemed to play a vital role in their continuing involvement or reengagement in congregations as young adults.

Through the stories interview participants related, it was clear they felt their adolescent congregations let them down at times, that adults in those congregations behaved in ways incongruent with the beliefs they espoused, that petty disagreements and selfishness sometimes got in the way. At the same time, these young adults found enough of the right stuff in the congregations of their youth to support them on their journey into adulthood shaped by faith.

2. For a fuller description of these interviews and my findings, see my book, *Reclaimed*, particularly chapters 3–7.

3. By "faithful fallowness," I describe a phenomenon from my research where emerging and young adults may appear not to have any involvement with a congregation, which can be assumed to mean they have rejected faith. In most cases in my research, this "fallowness" was actually a time of deepened inquiry and increased ownership of beliefs and practices, reflecting a deep "faithfulness" in the midst of seeming "fallowness."

In many cases where their own congregation fell short, those interviewed accessed other resources to provide what they perceived they needed, sometimes as a result of the networks those congregations provided. I also saw resilience in these young adults and in their faith such that they were able to stay the course when others their age did not, reminiscent to me of the emancipatory hope Evelyn Parker helpfully contrasts with wishful thinking.[4] Youth with resilience, driven by hope that frees them from that which threatens to restrain them, find paths and companions and alternate scripts in broken but "good enough" contexts. With a few assets, they are able to persist in assembling lives worth living into young adulthood.

"Good Enough" Churches, Hopeful Resilience, and A Faith Worth Living For

I made the assertion in *Reclaimed* that what youth and young adults are looking for—what their passion connects with most poignantly—is a *faith that's worth living for*, something they can be about in the world that's worth the investment of their lifetime. After all, adolescence can be a passionate time of life, full of energy, hope, possibilities, and 'why not?' questions. Of course, it can also be an overwhelming and anxiety-ridden time of existential despair that can rob one of hope. A faith worth living for offers the hope and security that other paths for meaning-making in adolescence have failed to offer. A faith worth living offers an alternate script to those promoted by other aspects of culture.

The life Jesus lived on earth was a passionate one throughout his brief years and was marked by the unquenchable hope fueled by a deep belief in one's mission. Jesus' life is one with which many youth and young adults connect in deep and life-giving ways. I would be remiss to draw too close a connection between the historic Jesus, an ancient Middle Eastern man deeply formed by his Jewish culture, and Christian adolescents today. Still, consider how Jesus sided with the marginalized while not "kissing up" to power brokers for his own personal gain—this is a key way in which Jesus' passion for justice connects with the adolescent drive for fairness and authenticity. From Jesus' passion for healing and wholeness to the love he showed to the least, the last, the lost, the little ones, and the lonely, it is evident that Jesus was consciously engaged in living his faith.[5] Even when

---

4. Parker. *Trouble Don't Last Always.*

5. In this brief description of Jesus' passionate life, I draw on the research of Jack

challenged by older and more powerful religious authorities, Jesus seemed guided by his own internal sense of vocation and voice—another example that adolescents and young adults will connect with.

Authentic qualities such as these that Jesus exemplified throughout his life are things all of us, but particularly young adults, wish we more fully embodied. Jesus' passionately faithful life is intriguing and inspiring—it connects with the passionate part of each of us.

Youth and young adults from my interviews thrived in contexts that made space for them to explore how their own passion connects with the world's greatest need at an intersection often referred to as vocation. Local congregations can be a place for this exploration *inasmuch as they remain open to the questions and critique youth and young adults uncover along their journey.*

For congregations that *can* manage the anxiety and discomfort that comes with the questioning and critiquing, the effect of youth and young adults' engagement is often life-affirming and generative. For those congregations that cannot manage the possibility of change in healthy ways—particularly for the youth and young adults in those congregations—the process can be painful and disruptive. Too many youth and young adults find themselves de-churched because their questions were not welcome, and too many congregations scratch their heads in befuddlement at what just transpired. Sadly, most do not realize what went wrong or fully appreciate their role in it.

Some young adults I interviewed, Morris and Tonya,[6] experienced this as young adults emerging into leadership in the congregation where Morris had grown up. Tonya questioned curricular and programming choices for youth and children on the Christian Education Committee, recommending relational and transformational emphases rather than those that were dogmatic and delivered through a 'schooling' method, but her questions were rejected out of hand. When her voice was squelched by those whose power mandated the changes in this and many other ways, Tonya and Morris both soon found their church home to be inhospitable. They no longer felt like "their" church—the church that was so much a part of their identities—was for them. Tonya and Morris eventually settled at another church, a place they describe as enlivened with questions in the

---

Seymour, *Teaching the Way of Jesus.*

6. Interviews with Morris and Tonya (pseudonyms) were first conducted as part of my doctoral dissertation at Garrett-Evangelical Theological Seminary.

midst of deep and real relationships. Tonya values the openness to questions for herself and Morris but even more so for her children as they reach adolescence.

One more thing worth noting: Tonya would be the first to say that when she was a younger adult she was still learning to speak up for herself, to use her growing sense of agency and voice. Sometimes, when she felt the most frustrated with the "powers that be" not listening to her, she was also frustrated with herself for not being able to make herself heard. Granted, some of it had to do with the disempowering actions of older adults, but it was also true that she simply wasn't very sure of herself yet—she wasn't as empowered as she is now. Another paradox emerges here when young adults use their emerging voices in the adult world and feel unheard. This is another time when paying attention more carefully and extending ample grace to one another goes a long way toward healing.

Tonya and Morris had sufficiently resilient faith to persist through all of this. After a period of being de-churched, they connected with others who were passionate about justice and mystery, the congregation in which they have raised their children and invested themselves. With "good enough" congregations and other support networks, Morris and Tonya's resilience or emancipatory hope steadied them as they grew into their voices and vocations.

Tribal Church

Some young adults, like Morris and Tonya, find congregations that do a "good enough" job of making space and fostering voice and vocation. The reality is that some do not. In her book, *Tribal Church: Ministering to the Missing Generation*, Carol Howard Merritt describes the circle of relationships to which people in the sometimes nomadic emerging adult subculture relate, calling it a tribe. In unpacking the term, "tribe," Merritt describes a group of people who gather around a common cause. She recognizes that most emerging adults first need basic care in the midst of the frequent turbulence that characterizes this period, things like a home-cooked meal and a listening ear or maybe even a place to stay for a couple of days when they are in-between apartments. Opportunities to share the practice of religious traditions (both historic and emerging traditions, not "the way we've always done it") is an important secondary value, followed by finding encouragement in an intergenerational network in the congregation. Contrasted with hollow habit, people can sense the transcendence and mystery of life-giving religious practices and are drawn to them. People need practices that help them tap into that transcendence and mystery, that help them remember who they are in the larger universe, that help them make meaning of life experiences. And people need relationships with others that are genuine—in their own generation and other generations.[7]

What Merritt describes as tribal church is, I believe, not nearly so new as is our awareness of it. Some describe the ongoing decline of church membership numbers as the decline of the Christian faith, but I believe we are overlooking important evidence to the contrary. Culturally we are experiencing a shift toward living one's Christian vocation with *or without* involvement in a formal congregation but surrounded and supported by a group that functions as a "tribe" or, I would contend, a group that becomes "church" in the most rudimentary meaning of the term. I see evidence of something akin to Merritt's tribal church existing outside formal congregations among my forty-something lesbian friends who were de-churched two decades ago because of their sexuality. I see it among fifty- and sixty-something colleagues who were de-churched because they didn't dress as expected or because they asked bold and honest questions decades ago. While, in each case, these folks may not have found a place in a congregation, they often did find a tribe that functions like church in their lives, sharing vision and passions, often also shaped by writings and music, empowering those within the tribe to live out their vocation, and working together to do good.

In recent interviews with emerging and young adults, I began to explore the ways in which they perceive that they "do good" of "do justice"—important aspects of my understanding of the church's work in the world—through their lenses. What I discovered was creative, passionate, and inspiring!

Living Vocation in the Tribe

Let me share with you the stories of five emerging and young adults who found ways to live out their God-given vocations in creative ways largely outside the church through their social service, social justice, and advocacy work. Those interviewed[8] in this round of investigations were all active in

7. Merritt. *Tribal Church*, 6–9.

8. Portions adapted from my article, "Young Adults 'Out-Front' in Engaging

mainline congregations as adolescents, but not all are now presently active in congregations today. In these young adults, I found passionate people engaged in acts of love and justice through their vocations, friendships, and communities.

- Judy went to law school intending to work in criminal prosecution or defense because she wanted to work for justice for those without a voice. Instead, she found herself drawn to bankruptcy law. In her work, Judy listens to people who are at the end of their ropes—people who have been taken advantage of by predatory creditors and payday lenders or who find themselves in generational poverty and need help making changes. She knows there are nonprofits and church-related organizations that speak to legislators or hand out food, but she wanted to help those most in need. A good listener who has always been passionate about helping others, Judy walks alongside the most vulnerable in our society as they make difficult decisions about bankruptcy, helping them feel hope and believe in themselves. Judy is still active in a congregation, but she sees her whole life as an opportunity to live out her Christian vocation.

- Lindsay works with compromised children in a mental health facility. She went into nursing to help people, and she chose this job in particular because it allows her to make a human connection with frequently overlooked children. She understands the dehumanizing aspects of care provided in a pediatric acute mental health facility, even in necessary procedures and precautions taken. Lindsay takes special joy in advocating for people whose lives are filled with abuse and pain. She is passionate about making sure they have the care they need to take positive next steps on a long road toward wholeness.

- Lindsay is involved in a congregation, but it is not a traditional kind of church. The child of a pastor, she developed a unique perspective on the extravagant waste of maintaining church buildings at the expense of helping hurting people. She is part of a faith community that intentionally has no building so resources are spent to help those in need with whom the congregation seeks to develop real relationships.

Outreach, Justice Ministries." *The Christian Citizen*, 1 (2014) 8-9. ©American Baptist Home Mission Societies, 2014. Used with permission. Portions later adapted in my book, *Reclaimed.* ©Judson Press, 2015. Used with permission.

- Daniel is an accountant with a major national firm who travels a lot on a rigorous work schedule. He spends his days identifying issues in corporations' financial systems and helping to ensure fair accounting practices. His work is important to him because he understands himself to be doing the right thing, the fair thing, on behalf of investors and employees of those corporations. Shaped by his upbringing in the church, Daniel now calls himself an agnostic but, in him, I saw someone who believes in the good humanity can do. When asked where he sees good in the world, he describes the way his partner inspires him with her kindness, grace, and passion to help others through her work as a medical professional. Daniel is a man of few words: "she makes me better" is how he describes the good he experiences from his relationship with his partner. In this I hear the near sacramentality I heard in the relationships other study participants in *Reclaimed* described with mentors and members of their congregations. Daniel's core beliefs are not inconsistent with the Christian faith of his younger years, but the incongruity of stated beliefs and lifestyle became too problematic for him. He lives his vocation with the support of family and a few close friends, driven by his passion for fairness and honor.

- Simone is a special education teacher in a middle school in an affluent suburb. She chose her work because it allows her to advocate for children considered incapable of doing many things. Using her voice on their behalf, she can help shape vocational and independent living options, plans that develop and begin to take shape in middle school. Simone is intentional about advising the classroom teachers about the unique abilities of each child and suggests educational strategies to help each student work to his or her highest level. Simone sees assets where others see deficiencies.

  Simone moved away from the church of her childhood as she struggled with its hypocrisy and authoritarian nature. The congregation of her adolescence helped exorcise some of her negative childhood experiences, but its current ministry just doesn't inspire her enough to compel her to attend. She and her husband have considered reconnecting with a church now that they have a young child, but she describes herself guided by her internal moral compass rather than by religious authorities. Community and hospitality are important to Simone, but church isn't the way she chooses to cultivate them.

- As a child, Michelle found herself befriending the special education children in the inclusion classroom in her elementary school. It was something of a personal crusade of hers to stop other kids from being mean to them. As an adult, she was intrigued by why the world didn't seem to be working for some children. She recently completed a master's degree in early childhood special education and works as a classroom teacher in a nonprofit preschool with children who have developmental delays that are further complicated by their impoverished home situations. She describes feeling drawn to early childhood special education because it seemed to her that the greatest impact could be made early in these children's lives. A passionate commitment to sharing God's love plays a role in Michelle's investment in this work, although she is not presently active in a congregation.

Michelle talks about living her faith through her work in this way: "I know that today, for the 3.5 hours I had my kids [in school], they knew they were safe, had the food they needed, and there were people to give them hugs even if they were throwing sand or cussing. . . . That's a good day. Even on the worst days, there's something good." Her colleagues at school and her family and friends have become the nurturing community from which she draws strength for living out her vision.

In the stories these emerging and young adults shared, I could not help but hear the ways their groups—their tribes or "churches"—aided in their meaning-making and passion for justice. I heard about music that provided the soundtrack of their lives and the ways it inspired and formed them. They told me about the stories and experiences that had become the lore of the group and, in some ways, paradigmatic of shared values and experiences. Much about their descriptions echoed aspects of the churches of their upbringing—those aspects that were life-giving and valuable to them. Their congregations were "good enough" in some ways and lacking in others at forming an identity in faith, creating space for real relationships, and fostering exploration of voice and vocation. When young adults like these opt out of church, congregations miss out on the gifts and perspectives of young adults like Judy and Simone, Daniel, Lindsay, Michelle, and many others. I'd like to believe these young adults and others like them would find their lives enriched by the beautiful tapestry of the Christian story and the rites and practices of the faith that help make meaning of life, as well.

Paying Attention to Grace: Building Redemptive Communities of Faith

It is my hope with this essay to elucidate a complicated issue faced by many congregations. In addition to reframing the problem, I will offer hopeful suggestions for companioning youth and young adults through this crucial life transition. In particular, my suggestions are directed toward religious educators whom I believe play an integral role in engaging younger and older members alike in redemptive living.

Relationships purposefully and intentionally full of grace and infused with the meaning of shared narrative can and do flourish in the churches all around these young adults—in "good enough" congregations that are doing their best. Congregations doing the hard work of paying attention, who are carefully exegeting the scriptures *and* their own lives and communicating across perceived barriers—these churches are unfortunately more the exception than the norm, but they do exist in varying degrees of "good enough." Passionate and compassionate young adults who are finding voice and vocation, who strive for justice and long for meaning—these folks are in communities everywhere, and they are also works-in-progress. I believe churches and young adults would benefit from connection with each other. I contend, in fact, that they *need* each other in key ways. I argue that responsibility for making the first move, for initiating reconciliation, rests with those with whom the greater power rests—most of the time, this means older and middle aged members of congregations.

In her chapter, "Staying Awake," in *Greenhouses of Hope*, Margaret Ann Crain describes a congregation that did something remarkable —and yet it should not be remarkable at all! First Church, described in her chapter, focused attention on its issues and assets and, over time, it became a better form of "good enough" in supporting the growth of youth and young adults both personally and in their faith. In the process of paying attention, "staying awake" to the God moments in their midst, the congregation learned and grew and changed. Aspects of how the congregation made meaning and understood itself shifted. For example, age alone was no longer one of the primary factors in identifying leadership when the congregation learned together that among its youth and young adults were gifts and talents the congregation needed. Based on her description, I assess that the congregation likely overlooked these gifted younger members, largely out of impatience with the evolving maturity of those youth and young adults in other areas. In the eyes of older and middle aged members, youth and young adults were the ones who were still developing and maturing when, in fact, those older and middle aged members were, too, whether or not they liked to admit it.[9]

If all humans are always growing, developing, and adapting (the most basic understand of human developmental theories), then paying attention means cultivating patience—even grace—with the ways each is in-process. In the Christian tradition, we have this sacrament (or gift, depending on your tradition) of grace. Grace, unmerited favor, serves as a constant reminder that we receive a gift which we cannot earn.

Paying attention to grace is, I believe, what the congregation in Crain's chapter was doing. When they did so, they came to see each other differently. Formed by this alternate narrative, the narrative of grace, those within the congregation came to see things from a new perspective. No longer were relationships defined solely by the capitalistic and individualistic culture—instead, relationships gradually were defined more and more by the alternate scripts of their faith tradition. As their corporate life was formed increasingly by these alternate scripts of faith—the first are last and the last are first, for example—the congregation became a place of abundance and thriving for more and more of those typically disenfranchised in the popular culture. What began happening at First Church as Crain describes it was not just window-dressing to attract young adults but rather a fundamental shift in how the church understood itself. This kind of paying attention replicated in congregations everywhere creates safe space for thriving and questioning for all but particularly those with less power and agency.

Paying attention, I would contend, also means congregations opening themselves to see those doing the work of love all around them and joining with them. Too many times, congregations draw rigid distinctions between those who are members and nonmembers, those inside and those outside of the church. Congregations use language that reinforces the idea that those inside are better, more spiritual—that those inside alone are the ones doing God's work. In my interviews I heard emerging and young adults tell a different story, offer an alternative narrative. Paying attention means taking first steps toward those who are doing good, initiating partnerships and crossing borders.

Remember the stories I told in my introduction to this chapter about Bethany and Marion? I imagine alternative narratives for the congregations

9. Crain, "Staying Awake."

where Bethany and Marion were hurt or ignored or stereotyped. I envision spaces filled with grace where genuine relationships make something truly amazing possible. I hope for people and places that pay attention to the deeper meaning of learning and growing together with one another. Bethany and Marion live all around us and, as their stories describe, may even be right next to us searching for meaning. Paying attention and extending the grace we have received is a first step toward congregations becoming redemptive communities across generations.

"The way is long—let us go together.

The way is difficult—let us help each other.

The way is joyful—let us share it.

The way is ours alone—let us go in love.

The way grows before us—let us begin."[10]

Bibliography

Crain, Margaret Ann. "Staying Awake." In *Greenhouses of Hope: Congregations Growing Young Leaders Who Will Change the World*. Dori Baker, ed. Lanham, MD: Rowman & Littlefield, 2010.

Janssen, Denise. *Reclaimed: Faith in an Emerging Generation*. Valley Forge: Judson, 2015.

Janssen, Denise. "Young Adults 'Out-Front' in Engaging Outreach, Justice Ministries." *The Christian Citizen* 1 (2014) 8–9. http://abhms.org/resources/christian_citizen/cc2014_1.cfm

Merritt, Carol Howard. *Tribal Church: Ministering to the Missing Generation*. Lanham, MD: Rowman & Littlefield, 2008.

Parker, Evelyn L. *Trouble Don't Last Always: Emancipatory Hope Among African American Adolescents*. Cleveland: Pilgrim, 2003.

Seymour, Jack L. *Teaching the Way of Jesus: Educating Christians for Faithful Living*. Nashville: Abingdon, 2014.

10. Attributed variously, often anonymously, but most commonly as a Zen Invocation.

_____ Afterword _____

Paying Attention and Pointing Forward

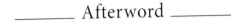

— *Margaret Ann Crain & Jack Seymour* —

THIS BOOK IS ABOUT the vocation of Christian religious education. It is about the role that the ministries of religious education can play in the complicated and challenging public worlds in which we live. For the faithful, education is essential – challenging the delusions that divide peoples and communities, pointing to the redemptive possibilities in the midst of life, and seeking to build coalitions of new life and hope that God's visions of healing and wholeness will come to be.

Can you guess our surprise when these colleagues in Christian education (all Garrett-Evangelical PhD graduates) told us they were planning this volume—and, moreover, even invited us to participate in it? Honestly, there are not words to express our appreciation. This collection of essays is deeply rooted in the commitments and vocations of all who have graduated from the program. They are making a difference—a redemptive difference—through seminary teaching, research, administration, church leadership, scholarship, and service in Korea, Malaysia, Africa, and the U.S. Above all, we thank Denise Janssen for her amazing editorial work.

We also thank our colleagues at Garrett-Evangelical who make it a place of faithful and mutual scholarship. We particularly recognize our colleagues in Christian religious education. Their shadows are throughout this volume—Linda Vogel, Reginald Blount, and Virginia Lee. Finally, we recognize President Neal Fisher who invited both of us to join the faculty of Garrett-Evangelical (10 years apart). Neal lives the commitment of connecting scholarship and teaching to the church and the culture.

"Redemptive community" – that is the good news of the Christian story. Lives can be transformed and societies can seek to fulfill God's vision of mutuality and justice where all are recognized as children of God. Jesus drew deeply on his Jewish heritage and its proclamation of God's steadfastness and vision of shalom for all people. Profoundly captured by Isaiah's image of the great banquet (Isaiah 25) when all would gather at God's table and the vision of a just community would be realized, Jesus in turn sponsored "great banquets" in each town that welcomed him.

While we know that vision and hope for a world of mutuality where all may thrive, brokenness and chaos intervene. Remember Jesus died on a Roman cross for seeking to point to redemptive living in the midst of Roman oppression. Many quaked in fear at Rome's power, turning away and hiding to save themselves. Later both his followers and the larger Jewish community were beaten, killed, and scattered by Roman military might.

Today, we also live in a world where fear is sewn by power. "Balancing budgets" is a euphemism for actions that destroy the safety net for the poor. In a world of scarcity—violence, suspicion, and racism rear their ugly heads. Systemic power seeks to consolidate its might and privilege, inflicting fear and causing people to turn away. Who will face forward, speak for inclusion, seek community, and hold up those who are being broken? Honestly that is what living redemptively is all about – challenging the forces that destroy lives and restrict the thriving of creation – all creation. God's vision is one of abundance where the good that God created in persons and all the earth can release hope and possibilities. Redemption is the life force of God's world!

The authors of this volume seek in different ways and places to point to possibilities of redemption. Look at their ministries: nurturing vocation, mentoring new life, providing institutions that promote life chances, crossing cultures, calling for a global vision, working with persons who are outcast and in jail, and welcoming the voices of all into dialogue about God's vision of new life and hope.

They offer us clues—to name a few:

- Listen deeply to the realities of people's lives,
- Seek to build communities of mutual learning,
- Attend to in-breaking moments of new life,
- Teach spiritual practices,
- Challenge injustice,
- Build constituencies,
- Call institutions to faithfulness,

- Provide mentoring and nurturing relationships,

- Honor the God-given goodness and gifts of all,

- Persistently pursue "redeemability," and

- Above all, connect faith to living.

The *content* of the Christian message, its good news, is that new life is possible—people and communities and the world can be redeemed. The *method of teaching* is, in fact, to live redemptively. Redemptive living begets redemptive living.

In the midst of all of our limitations and failures, in the midst of forces of power and privilege, in the midst of intra- and inter-religious conflict, proclaim that God is indeed making a difference. Teach that we all are called to be partners in building, as we can, where we can, communities and institutions of hope. New life is possible, mutual living is possible, and the flourishing of creation is possible.

Our colleagues call us to work where we are and as we are able, to point to God's redeeming activity, and to build constituencies of hope. In amazing moments, often where we do not expect it, new life breaks through and possibilities are launched. Follow them. We hope you'll join in living and educating for redemptive community. This must be the focus of the field of Christian religious education, for this work is crucial to the flourishing of community and the enacting of hope.